WIRED to Hear

CONNECTING GOD'S VOICE TO
YOUR LIFE, INFLUENCE, AND CAREER

SHAWN BOLZ | BOB HASSON

D0194405

Copyright © 2021 by Shawn Bolz and Bob Hasson

All rights reserved, including the right of reproduction in whole or in part in any form. No portion of this book may be reproduced in any form whatsoever, except for brief quotations in reviews, without the written permission.

Published by ICreate Productions,
PO Box 50219, Studio City, CA 91614
www.bolzministries.com

To contact the author about speaking at your conference or church,
please go to www.bolzministries.com

Unless otherwise noted, all Scripture quotations are from the New International Version®. NIV®. Copyright © 1973, 1978, 1984, 2011 by Biblica, Inc.™ Used by permission of Zondervan. All rights reserved worldwide. www.zondervan.com. Scripture quotations identified NASB are taken from the New American Standard Bible®. Copyright © 1960, 1962, 1963, 1968, 1972, 1973, 1975, 1977, 1995 by The Lockman Foundation. Used by permission. www.Lockman.org Scripture quotations marked TPT are from The Passion Translation®. Copyright © 2017, 2018 by Passion & Fire Ministries, Inc. Used by permission. All rights reserved. ThePassionTranslation.com. Scriptures marked KJV are taken from the Holy Bible, King James Version, public domain. Scriptures marked ESV are taken from the Holy Bible, English Standard Version®. Copyright© 2001 by Crossway, a publishing ministry of Good News Publishers. Scripture quotations identified NLT are from the Holy Bible, New Living Translation®. Copyright © 1996, 2004, 2015 by Tyndale House Foundation. Used by permission of Tyndale House Publishers, Inc., Carol Stream, Illinois, 60188. All rights reserved. Scripture quotations marked MSG are taken from The Message, copyright © 1993, 1994, 1995, 1996, 2000, 2001, 2002 by Eugene H. Peterson. Used by permission of NavPress. All rights reserved. Represented by Tyndale House Publishers, Inc. Scripture quotations identified KJ21 are from the Holy Bible, 21st Century King James Version® (KJ21®). Copyright ©1994 by Deuel Enterprises, Inc., Gary, SD 57237. All rights reserved. Scripture quotations identified NKJV are from the New King James Version®. Copyright © 1982 by Thomas Nelson, Inc. Used by permission. All rights reserved. Scriptures marked GNB are taken from the Good News Bible®. Copyright © 1994 by the Bible Societies/Harper-Collins Publishers Ltd UK, Good News Bible© American Bible Society 1966, 1971, 1976, 1992. Scriptures marked ERV are taken from the Holy Bible, Easy-to-Read Version © 2001 by World Bible Translation Center, Inc. Used by permission. Scriptures marked AMP are taken from the Holy Bible, Amplified Bible Copyright © 1954, 1958, 1962, 1964, 1965, 1987, 2015 by the Lockman Foundation. Used by Permission. www.Lockman.org

Paperback ISBN: 978-1-952421-15-0
eBook ISBN: 978-1-952421-16-7
Printed in the United States of America

Table of Contents

Introduction

"Marketplace leaders are going to be the fore-runners in the next great move of God."

Shawn Bolz, 2019

In 2018, God gave me an impression that marketplace people are going to be the focus of the next move of God that will bring millions into the Kingdom.

He is going to use believers in the marketplace as the front-liners to culture. That means the stakes are really high and the war is very great, so we can't go after this in our own strength, wisdom, or power. We must build with spiritual tools so we can bear natural fruit that has spiritual implications over lives.

We need the courage to trust and hear God in our careers, businesses, and finances—not just as an occasional occurrence when God disrupts our big decisions, but as a way of life in all things, partnering with God in our practical daily decisions.

It's time to access the fullness of what He has made available to you in your lifetime through hearing His voice. Our mission is simple; we need to hear God. Let's partner with His incredible wisdom and grace and from that place, do the work He has called us to do.

When I talked to Bob Hasson about writing this book with me, I processed with him about how I believe we are wired in our spiritual DNA to hear God's voice and the thoughts I had about people in careers, business owners, entrepreneurs, and people who work in all kinds of occupations. Bob was in agreement, but even more, he carries such a practical wisdom about hearing God in the marketplace.

We started to record some of our conversations, which became the birthplace of this very book. We have also created an ongoing conversation through our podcast, Exploring the Marketplace, where we meet with career people to discuss their relationship with God and how He meets them in their careers and provides a feeling of connectedness that we were created for. We host this on the Charisma Podcast Network and hope you will join us there!

Bob and I have been in relationship for many years and began to travel together teaching on God in the marketplace and hearing God outside of the Church. Our lives blend well between Bob's practical wisdom and my understanding of teaching others to hear God.

Bob has been in the church and in business for over forty years. He has served on church boards for over thirty years and is the co-author of *The Business of Honor* with Danny Silk.

I have been in ministry now since 1994, but alongside that, I have worked in the video game and film and TV industry for over fifteen years and have consulted with businesses and nonprofits for half of my life. I have written a large number of books; worked as a freelance journalist; spoken all around the world at events, conferences, conventions, and churches; and am a TV and podcast host. I even founded a church in L.A. and pastored it for over a decade. The church is still going strong with its new senior pastors and it is where I attend to this day. My experience in senior pastoring, prophetic ministry, and owning my own businesses has taught me to thrive in organizational leadership and has given me a unique perspective that I hope will help you.

We've come together to help infuse you with hope, truth, and perspective about your God-given role in the marketplace. Whether you own or manage a business, have spent decades in your career, or are simply trying to find value in the work that you do, this book is for you.

God has hardwired you to partner with Him and to hear Him in all areas of your life. Hearing God is not just an esoteric or philosophical experience reserved for a church service. Instead, His voice should create faith that can change the metrics of industries, shift the bottom line for the poor, and cause leaders and influencers to wonder about who it is you serve. Your partnership with God should bring solutions to industries that have given up hope of changing or evolving. It should cause big industries to see huge shifts toward a better future.

As Christians, we can all believe together that when God appoints His people within the culture, it is going to bring transformation. Isaiah prophesied in Isaiah 9:7 that the government that would be placed on Jesus' shoulders would never end. We should expect the government of Jesus to increase in visible ways. The world has millions of problems and it is the glory of God to bring solutions. His glory is seen in the love that manifests not only through salvation but also in how He brings blessing and solutions in the practical areas of our lives.

It was God's original intent to share His mind with us. Adam and Eve walked with God in the garden, discovering His creation and exploring His mind and purposes. While that connection was lost with the Fall, Jesus restored us to that full relationship and connection that He Himself had: a place of communion with God. First Corinthians 2:16 reminds us that we *have* the mind of Christ. We have access to hear God's heart for humanity, government, city infrastructure, education, and every area of our lives.

Throughout the book, we make reference to King Solomon as a spiritual prototype for hearing and revealing God in the marketplace. Solomon heard God and then implemented that revelation to lead and develop his kingdom.

Not only did Solomon use the wisdom of God to build the temple, but he also developed infrastructure, government, craftsmanship, and the very mindset of Israel and its people. Second Chronicles 9:22 says that King Solomon was greater in riches and wisdom than all the other kings of the earth. His kingdom was also a place where the people were at peace. While David was often at war with surrounding kingdoms, Solomon's reign brought political peace.

In many ways, this was a prototype for the future. It was the first Messianic picture and how many Israelites thought the Messiah would transform the earth. But Jesus came to impart a Kingdom that would last forever, not an earthly kingdom that would fade away. Yet, through Solomon, we glimpse a revelation that comes fully into focus in Christ: God seeks to partner with us to redeem the earth. In everything we do, we have access to God's heart and mind, His solutions for every problem, His unconditional love for every human, and His passion for the very earth itself.

It all starts with hearing His voice. As we walk with God, we become conduits of His resource, blessing, and provision, but for a purpose: transformation of hearts, cultures, cities, and even the climate. Many lose sight of that purpose while crafting their career or business or simply working hard to create resources, finances, or wealth.

As you read this book, we hope that the way we describe hearing God will feel familiar to you. Instead of spiritualizing your role and place in the marketplace, we want to demystify what it looks like to hear God and do the work He has called you to do.

As you walk this journey with us, you'll have an opportunity to build spiritually driven goals for both your own career as well as the industry you are called to. Throughout the book, we explore real-life examples of what it looks like to hear God and follow His leading within marketplace roles. We also discuss where our understanding of God, Church, and the marketplace has been immature or broken. The goal is that you are empowered to do it differently.

Lastly, we want to charge you to feel fully appointed, commissioned, and empowered to do what you are called to in an intentional, God-driven way.

You have been given powerful tools to make a difference in your life and the lives of those around you.

It is time to gain a hope-filled view of the ways in which you already hear from God about your life and the work of your hands, and explore the things He is saying to you, for the sake of the world.

Shawn Bolz

CHAPTER 1

Hear

"I don't hear from God." Shawn's friend, who is one of the more successful businessmen he knows, looked at him with utter conviction. "My wife is that kind of person," he said. "I wish I did, though, because things would be so much easier."

"Mark, I can prove to you in about fifteen minutes that over the course of the last twenty years, you have been following the voice of God but have not understood it. You are wired to hear from Him. He made you that way."

"Fine, try me," he said.

Shawn remembered how much Mark always talked about his three adult children and how much he loved them. "What was the largest financial sacrifice you made for one of your children and why?" Shawn asked.

"That's easy. My son and now daughter-in-law were getting married, and we gave them enough money from their inheritance to buy their dream home."

"That doesn't sound like a normal decision. What compelled you to do that?" Shawn asked.

"Well, he met her in a mission organization, and she was from a third-world country. She had never owned a home nor had her family. She is highly educated and only wanted a career. My wife and I felt that if they had a house, they would feel able to start a family."

"And what happened?" Shawn asked.

"She loved having a home! They got pregnant in their first year. We now have three grandbabies after five years of their marriage and she loves it so much she was able to transition her career from full time to contract work."

"How did you come to that decision? That was a huge sacrifice and very generous. Did your other kids get jealous or misunderstand?"

"Well, we were praying in a room we have designated as a prayer room, and the idea came to me. And no, our other kids love her and were in full support."

"So, you were just praying, and an idea jumped into your head?"

"I mean, I know what you are saying but I didn't hear a voice. I didn't even feel a tingle."

"But you made a decision that changed the trajectory of their lives, freed them up to pursue legacy over career, helped them to embrace the identity of family, and you are the hero of this story?" Shawn laughed, not really rebuking him, but enjoying his realization of God's voice in his life.

"Oh ..." Mark started to ponder.

"Your instinct is beautiful. Your ability to hear is powerful. You need to stop looking for an external voice to lead you and trust that Jesus sent His Holy Spirit to live inside of you, and this is the fruit of that relationship."

Shawn and Mark began to reverse engineer several other times when there was great fruit in his life in business and family. Through this process, he found God's voice.

Wired to Hear God's Voice

God wants to talk to us more than we desire to hear Him. In fact, when we begin to reverse engineer big decisions, blessings, and moments of impact, like Mark did, we can start to recognize how God speaks to us in our everyday lives. We also begin to see how we are created not just to hear His voice but also to know His heart.

It's important to note that hearing from God is not always a direct route to solving our problems or helping us succeed. Communication is not just transactional; it's relational. Usually when we are desperate enough to pursue God's voice, it is when we have pain, problems, or issues, and we come wanting God to fix something or accomplish our agenda.

God has an agenda as well: to walk with us, share the way He processes, show us what is available, and give us results for our lives that couldn't be realized without Him. God created us for relationship. Just like in any relationship, communication is essential to our connection with God, which means He created us with the express desire to commune with us.

> But God now unveils these profound realities to us by the Spirit. Yes, he has revealed to us his inmost heart and deepest mysteries through the Holy Spirit, who constantly explores all things. After all, who can really see into a person's heart and know his hidden impulses except for that person's spirit? So it is with God. His thoughts and secrets are only fully understood by his Spirit, the Spirit of God. (1 Corinthians 2:10-11, TPT)

In 1 Corinthians, Paul paints a picture of the importance of relationship in hearing God's voice. The Holy Spirit searches the depths of the Father's heart, the same Father who prepared us for works before time began. The Father who provides better than any natural father ever could and who has plans to prosper us. The Father who says, "Call to Me and I will show you unimaginable things that you can't ever see without looking through My heart." The Father who has dreams for us that are beyond what we could hope for or imagine (see Ephesians 3:20).

God is dreaming over and guiding humanity all the time, but He also does more than speak to us; He gives us His nature, mind, and heart.

In 1 Corinthians 2:15-16, Paul goes on to explain to the church of Corinth that no one really knows the amazing things God has in store for humankind except for us—we know it by God's own Spirit, because we have the mind of Christ: "Those who live in the Spirit are able to carefully evaluate all things, and they are subject to the scrutiny of no one *but God.* For who has ever intimately known the mind of the Lord Yahweh well enough to become his counselor? *Christ has,* and we possess Christ's perceptions" (TPT).

Beyond giving us His mind, nature, and revelation of His heart, we are also given the gifts of the Holy Spirit—powerful tools that all believers have access to use. Paul told the church of Corinth to pursue love and eagerly desire the gifts, especially prophecy (see 1 Corinthians 14:1), because these things are available to everyone. The gifts of the Spirit are the tools that help us to realize what is in God's heart for us and the world around us.

As the Holy Spirit searches the innermost depths of God's heart, He then places His thoughts, His dreams, and His truth inside of our spirits prophetically. He wires us to know what is in His heart. Much like a husband and wife learn to communicate and share their thoughts through little interactions, expressions, and gentle promptings, the Holy Spirit teaches us how to have a connection with God where we simply know and understand His heart.

Hearing God in the Marketplace

God's dreams, plans, and purposes are not only for us but also for every environment and industry: science, government, healthcare, and so on. His dreams are also for things we don't even know are coming.

Not only are we wired to hear His voice and know His heart for our own life, but He also wants to take our ability to hear His voice to another level so that we can grow and expand our positions in the marketplace.

When we don't expect God's voice in the midst of our daily lives or careers, then we become task driven and try to do things *for* Him rather than partnering *with* Him. If we don't expect to hear God's voice, it can violate the people we are called to serve.

The goal of hearing God in our everyday lives is not to evangelize every moment but to walk with God in connection. As we do, we begin to see God's grace and influence in everything. This, in turn, creates a demonstration of His love to the world around us.

An early church father, Francis of Assisi, preached a similar message. Whether this is a true story or just a picture of his life, we don't know, but it still demonstrates a truth he walked out. The story goes that a priest said to St. Francis, "I don't see you preach often." St. Francis, who had determined to preach the gospel through the literal demonstration of the great commission, looked around at all that he had accomplished and said, "I preach Christ daily and sometimes use words."

Francis considered all nature to be a reflection of God. He was the most accomplished minister of his time, gathering crowds; but instead of preaching directly, he invited them to participate in tasks such as gardening or feeding the poor. His followers, often the children of wealthy lords and ladies, weren't used to slowing down and looked at farming as menial work not fit for the educated. But they went to him in droves and detoxed the worldliness that was their priority system and became true believers grounded in the Kingdom—all because St. Francis heard God's voice and chose to demonstrate His love where the people were: in the streets.

God never limited His voice to building churches or the religious expression of Christianity. The Bible is full of stories of God speaking to people, prophets, and leaders about their concerns when it comes to the marketplace, government, creativity, and every area of life. As a matter of fact, much of what God spoke to the people of Israel had to do with stewardship of their communities, natural affairs, and businesses.

We see this in Jesus' interactions with the disciples—telling them where to cast their nets in order to bring in a large catch of fish—as well as in the Old Testament. In 1 Samuel 9, Saul's father sends Saul in search of some missing donkeys. The donkeys are part of the family's business, their livelihood and legacy. When Saul can't find the donkeys, he and his father's servant seek the voice of God through the prophet Samuel. Not only does God answer Saul's need, but He also redirects Saul toward a bigger picture beyond just the family business.

People hear from God about the things that are most important to humanity because God cares about everything: finances, resources, social equality, branding, personal struggles, family, politics, social justice—all of it. Several of Jesus' miracles involved speaking to the disciples about resources and finances: a widow's mite, a prophetic word on where to get money for taxes, a rich man who wouldn't truly sacrifice, the lilies of the field and birds of the air who were always provided for. God speaks about resources and work all the time.

A few years ago, Bob went on a journey of discovering God's heart to speak to us within the marketplace and not just the church. He learned that God's love never fails, even in business. At the time, he was writing his first book with Danny Silk, called *The Business of Honor*, which was based on Danny's revolutionary *Culture of Honor* book. The premise, and the main point Danny was trying to make, was that doing business as a Christian is all about love; love is a business tool. But Bob, an experienced businessman, disagreed. He wrestled with the idea of using the word "love" in the context of business.

In 2017, during the college national championship game, Clemson upset Alabama to win their first college football championship game since 1981. In an interview after the game, Clemson coach Dabo Swinney said, "I told them [the team] tonight that the difference in this game would be the love they have for each other." Bob began to realize how our connection to God's voice and heart can impact everything we touch. He understood that if he is bent toward the Father, then everyone he comes into contact with will experience the love of the Father, no matter the context of their meeting.

As he began exploring this concept, he also discovered that he had actually been building his business with this identity and culture of love all along. He simply hadn't viewed it that way. As a business owner, he knew that he loved what he was building and who he was building. Bob has hundreds of employees that come from all kinds of backgrounds, and his goal is (and always has been) to create a healthy workspace full of honor. He worked hard to make his company the best company it could be, bearing in mind the welfare of his employees. The feedback he received from his employees proved that he was setting the right goals and that they could feel how much he cared for them.

Bob had partnered with God's heart for his business from the beginning; he just didn't fully recognize God's voice in the midst of all his business decisions. When he reverse engineered the decisions he had made and the fruit he could see in his company, it was clear how God had guided his business.

How Do I Hear God?

If hearing from God is so easy, and if it is true that we are wired to hear His voice, then why do many of us still struggle to recognize His guidance in our daily lives?

The hardest initial part of this connection with God is learning the unique way that He speaks to *you*. Learning to recognize God's voice in our everyday lives is different from learning to hear with our physical ears. John 10:27 says, "My own sheep will hear my voice, and I know each one, and they will follow me" (TPT). Throughout scripture, we see that hearing God's voice requires us to listen with our spiritual ears.

Jesus clearly demonstrated the importance of intimacy and hearing God's voice. He regularly took time away to be with the Father, and He told His disciples more than once that He only did what He saw and heard the Father do and say (see John 5:19). He was in constant communication with God.

Likewise, the more we pray, read the Bible, and learn how to listen with our spiritual ears, the more we will find continual, tangible input from the heart of God—input that changes the way we approach life, relationships, and even our careers.

Consider the last time you experienced a success that came from either a great idea, a gut instinct, or simply a heart to help or serve. Reverse engineer that experience until you find the moment that first led you down that path toward success. Can you find God's voice in the midst of your story?

For most people, there is no audible voice or open vision when God speaks. His guidance comes in much more subtle, and sometimes in very specific, ways. In John 15, God promised to abide in us and work from within, communicating to us intimately and personally—not only that, but He also sent the Holy Spirit to help guide and encourage us. This means that our instinct, our gut, our internal dialogue within our spirit man is one of the ways God communicates and processes with us.

One of the biggest obstacles we face isn't a lack of communication from God but a failure to acknowledge and give God the credit. When many of us experience big wins in life that come from listening to our inner voice or instinct, we celebrate as if we are the hero of the story.

When we learn to see our wins in life, our greatest successes, through spiritual eyes, we can reverse engineer how we got there. What made you follow that path? What prompted you to have that thought? There, in the midst of gut decisions and seemingly random ideas, is God's voice.

Of all the people we have trained to hear from God, we've come to see that the number one way that He speaks is from within, or through impressions. God speaks to us through our inner thought life—something that is so normal for us. His voice can be heard often, but we have to get observant enough to distinguish His voice from our own thoughts.

We can start by valuing and treasuring the way God speaks to us. Recognizing the internal process of hearing His voice confirms that this eternal Trinity is working within our being to form His nature. His voice should be precious to us. As we learn what our thoughts are and what His thoughts are, and place value on His thoughts over our own, we grow in our ability to recognize His voice. To discern between the two is when we really start to mature.

Learning to recognize God's voice through your inner thought life helps you recognize Him in other ways as well. God is always speaking, and how He speaks changes and sometimes depends on our willingness to listen. These are a few of the ways in which we see God speak throughout scripture. Take some time to consider this list and note how and when God has spoken to you using any of the following methods:

Ways God Speaks

(excerpt from *Modern Prophets*, p. 84)

- ¤ Dreams: Job 33:14-15
- ¤ Visions: Daniel 4:4-37; Acts 9:12; 16:9-11
- ¤ Angels: Psalm 91:11
- ¤ Trances: Acts 11:4-5; 10:9-11
- ¤ Impressions: Mark 2:8-12
- ¤ The Audible and "Still Small Voice" of God: Luke 9:35; Isaiah 30:21
- ¤ Memories: John 14:26; Mark 8:18; Psalm 77:11
- ¤ Flashbacks: Genesis 28:13; Habakkuk 3:2
- ¤ Divine Revelations: Luke 24:45
- ¤ Scents/Smells: 2 Corinthians 2:14
- ¤ Divine Translation/Transportation: Acts 8:39-40; 2 Kings 5:26
- ¤ Thoughts: 1 Corinthians 2:16
- ¤ Visitations: Revelations 1:12-17

Hear God; Do Work

We all have the ability to hear God in our jobs and daily life, even when it's not a Christian environment. Knowing God's voice means we have access to consistent divine help in the midst of complex dynamics in our industries, because we get to process with God's Spirit.

In business, for example, when someone has a huge success or doubles their budget, they also begin to face things like disgruntled employees or under-talented staff and must learn to resolve those issues. When clients come to us with a challenging job or we experience an unexpected obstacle at work, we get to seek God's wisdom and hear His voice in order to discover out-of-the-box solutions. Then it is up to us to change our position and take whatever steps we can to activate what we are hearing.

Learning to hear God, even in the mundane moments of life, can radically change our perspective of God's plan and purposes for our lives. Then we can continue to build off of those moments to create a lifestyle of intentional relationship with God. By tapping into a deeper relationship with God and believing that we are called to walk with Him and hear His voice, we can have an impact on the world that no generation of Christians has had before.

ACTIVATION

1. What is one story in your life when you felt the gentle nudge of God's voice?
2. Think of a tremendous victory in your life and reverse engineer the story to see how God was the author of that victory.
3. Do a quick search on Solomon and identify how he processed with God. Can you recall any time wisdom or revelation came to you for something practical in your life?
4. What is one pressing issue that you have? Ask God to speak to you about it and open your spiritual ears to hear Him in a new and different way. Write down what you hear.

CHAPTER 2

Work

In order to write a book about God's plan and purpose in the marketplace, we must understand His perspective on work. As a Church, we have often devalued the role of Christians in the marketplace (not to mention the skills that put them in those roles). God, however, has a different perspective on "work" and "ministry" than what many of us have come to understand.

In the beginning, God told Adam and Eve to steward the earth. They were in a connected, face-to-face relationship with Him. They did not need temples, worship services, or roles to show them who they were to God and how to worship or relate to Him. Everything they did was in Him; it was spiritual. Naming the animals, tending the gardens, loving each other—it was all what they were designed for and it was perfect.

We have stepped far away—in our Judeo-Christian mindset—from how He made us in the beginning. Christians today may not recognize how little "Church service" time there is in heaven. We are not going to a big prayer meeting in the sky for eternity; we are going to be with God and to work with Him on everything that is His.

In the New Testament, Jesus says in John, "My Father and I are always working" (John 5:17 paraphrase). It is an interesting concept that

Jesus was always working and still is now. Then, in the upper room, He gave the disciples an assignment to work as well. It was their job to go and change the world and to build His Church. Who were His disciples? All career people: fishermen, laborers, workers—every last one of them. We were created to work.

The Work of Restoration

Our job, the work set before us, is to steward the Kingdom here and now. We are commissioned to do the work of restoration. Ephesians 2:10 (TPT) says, "Even before we were born, God planned in advance *our destiny* and the good works we would do *to fulfill it!*" We understand our destiny to be there for the people we love, and the good works are the calling or career or passionate things we do that help us to love them.

Yet, John 3:16 says, "For God so loved the world." When we begin to love what God created—and not just the people around us—with His eyes and heart, we see how wonderful He made it. The Hebrews understood that God loved the world. Many modern Christians are taught or just inherently think that the world is going to burn and go to hell, so what's the point of pursuing a career outside of ministry and saving souls?

When we interpret "For God so loved the world" to only mean humanity—not industry or culture, not animals or science—then everything that is not centered around our visible connection to people for God, and worshiping God, has no value. We miss the whole picture that God made the world and rested in His love for it. He loves the *world*, and humanity is the trophy in the center of that love, but Jesus came to redeem and restore *all things*.

This truth should impact everything we do. In our careers, no matter the industry, we are doing the work of restoration. If we recognized what it means to really walk with God and hear His voice for the world around us, we should have tangible solutions to huge problems in society, agriculture, and science. We have the power, right now, to heal land through agriculture. We have the power to eliminate harmful plastics with new technology that can biodegrade.

We were given the power to rule and reign and do the work of restoration, so why aren't we? Our current Christian culture does not promote this type of stewardship, and in many cases, we do not expect to hear God's voice for solutions and ideas outside of our own personal needs.

Our ability to do the work God has called us to do is connected to our choice to hear and recognize His voice. In many ways, the reason we do not know we hear from God is that we are not in touch with the things He's talking about. We do not even know that He cares about those things.

Yet, the more we hear from God, the more we can accomplish in the natural. The more we hear His voice, the more we care about things that our own limited experiences or minds would not even think about. Little convictions turn into huge hope for change and Kingdom perspective to see where God is making the most tangible impact. Do we care about how something as simple as spitting our gum out the window can impact the earth? When we start to connect to God's voice, we discover a passion for the earth, the environment, and all living things. We begin to understand God's heart to restore and redeem all things.

God's Value System

Being spiritually adopted by God into the Kingdom is a lot like becoming a citizen of a new nation. If you became an American today, for the first time, you would have to learn what your freedoms are and why they are so valuable. The same is true of the Kingdom of God. We need to learn what God's intentions are for His Kingdom, how He designed it, and what role we play in that design. Suddenly, from this place of understanding, the work we accomplish every day becomes far more valuable in our own eyes.

One of the reasons we commonly hold ministry above work in the marketplace is due to dualism. It is the belief that everything that is natural is not spiritual. That means the natural world is not as valuable as everything that is spiritually focused. This causes Christians, for example, to hate music that is not faith focused. Love songs can even be looked at as evil because of who wrote them or what they are about, even if they are pure. Dualism is a common religious attitude we are still detoxing from 2,000 years after Jesus was raised from the dead.

Can you imagine the God who commanded that we love Him, our neighbor, and ourselves, and who loves romance, commanding us to avoid the beauty of romance through music? What if you and your spouse were not allowed to have a song you share as a couple because it looked humanistic or unspiritual? The reality is, we should think about our spouses in every good love song, and they help us to honor the command of the Bible.

Think of it this way: Let's say your daughter draws a beautiful picture of your family, then your house, and then her dogs and chickens and cat. Then she draws the sky and the trees and the nature around it, then lastly draws herself holding her favorite toys that you bought her.

Then let's say you come and cut out the picture of the family and crumple up the rest in front of her and throw it away. She would be devastated and would ask, "Why did you do that to my picture? I feel so sad. You didn't like my picture?" And she would be heartbroken because you violated the full picture in order to preserve only the part that you think is valuable.

But every part of that picture is valuable to God: the nature that He designed, the house to be built, the atmosphere, the animals He gave as pets, the toys the parents bought the child, the house itself, and the family. Yes, only the family goes to heaven with the identity that was formed by the way they lived the gospel out on the very real earth.

This is how a lot of Christians treat life and especially work. We cut out what we think is important to God and make everything else feel less important, even insignificant.

God sees the way the Church is treating everything other than the inherently spiritual purposes. We imagine Him saying, "I can't talk to them because they're seeing one aspect of what I talk about. They do not see how much I love science. I love technology. I love creativity. I love it all. That is all My nature on the earth. There are certain ways of connecting to Me that I have hidden in careers that can only be seen through jobs. They can only be seen through the marketplace and will be eternal." In order to fully step into the work God has called us to, we must inherit His value system and His heart of restoration.

Changing the Marketplace Relationship to the Church

Part of understanding how much God values the work we accomplish, and why the marketplace calling is so significant, is also understanding the relationship between the church and the marketplace.

For some reason, in our modern Christianity, marketplace-focused Christians often feel secondary to those around them who lead entirely within the organized church structure. Many times, a church's operational structure or core beliefs are not balanced, and those in business are the perfect people to help with that. Yet, business leaders and marketplace influencers aren't invited into those conversations or looked at as an asset or resource within the church. Instead, the church makes the mistake of marginalizing people who create finances to just be that: donors. So many times we see people who are running high-level businesses and multibillion-dollar corporations all the way down to mom-and-pop small businesses who have no voice in the church because they are not in ministry.

The interesting thing about marketplace entrepreneurs and business managers or owners is that they have most of the talents that the church needs with respect to organization and the practicality with respect to leading. But the unspoken rules of Christianity communicate that influence, vision, and purpose must be built around people and salvation. For marketplace leaders, often their vision is built around mission. This focus on bringing people through the church doors is creating a vacuum of church failure, evident in the statistics showing the decline of churches.

If we look at what God is doing, however, we are seeing a new breed of thinkers and builders emerging who have ingenuity and understand God's value system. Instead of separating church and marketplace wisdom, an emerging generation of church leaders are taking new approaches to work and spirituality and building businesses and sources of income within their churches and cities.

For example, we know of a businesswoman who partnered with her pastor and became the "builder" for the church. She reviews financial statements, put together a strategic plan, organized a building campaign, and recruits high-net-worth donors. Within this relationship, the pastor made a choice to trust this woman, and this marketplace leader had to learn that the realities of business sometimes did not apply within the church world.

The relationship between the church and marketplace is also changing in other ways. A friend of ours who is an expert in financial planning organized and began to teach classes within the church environment, setting people free who were struggling with finances. The church typically is not equipped to discuss such practical matters.

We believe that we are on the precipice of a transformation within the marketplace *and* the church. The age that we live in with the technology that we have and the ability to get information at the touch of a finger is an invitation to blend marketplace leadership within the church. We have begun to see marketplace leaders blessed by the church, empowered by the church, and released by the church. The same is true of the marketplace acceptance of church, as we have seen pastors hired for certain corporations as spiritual counselors or chaplains or on the boards of large companies to bring their spiritual views.

What Is Your Role in the Local Church?

We are wired for community, and while most of us are called to the marketplace, some of the most beautiful connections and times of ministry will happen through our Christian connections. Being part of your local church is a significant way to build community and participate in what God is doing through the lives of others.

While our value for work is changing, and the relationship between the church and the marketplace is growing, it can still be challenging to understand our roles in the church when we feel called to the marketplace. Part of walking in connection to God's voice is listening to Him about our roles in the context of the church we go to and the ministries we are involved with.

One of the big complaints of those called to the marketplace who get involved in churches is feeling as though their contribution is less significant and not knowing how to balance church life and work life. They can see that ministry-minded people value them, mostly because they are providers. Generosity is expected and sought out, but their voice and history in the marketplace, along with education, work experience, or cultural influence, become extremely secondary to the spiritual work of Christianity.

In church, we can put the highest-skilled person in a position of stacking chairs and never promote them or utilize them for what they carry. In ministry, a lot of the strategy and structure is undefined, and this creates a ton of roles to be filled and a mentality of all-hands-on-deck. That is normal in business startups as well, but in startups you cannot use unskilled people for too long, and overly skilled people will not stay in an under-qualifying or underpaying role for too long either. Serving is the core of all Christian ministries and this is vital, but when it is done in a way that marginalizes someone, this is dishonoring and counterproductive.

As church leaders, we should be looking at the people who are coming to our churches and then investigate who they are and really see what they are called to bring, even if they don't have forty hours a week to volunteer. Part of what we have seen is that, as people discover who their ministry family and audience are and learn how to take risks and trust them, they begin to build something greater than they first envisioned. There is a broadening of the scope of calling for both the church leaders and the marketplace professionals.

It is important to be involved in church community because we are part of one body. Our gifts and talents are needed both in our careers and in church. However, as we ask God what our role is within the church, it is helpful to have a clear vision. If we don't have a clear vision and purpose for why we are participating with a specific ministry, then they will definitely define one for us. Sometimes they won't even tell us, as it's just part of their ministry culture. This can lead to misunderstandings and even delay in our God-given assignments. Meaning, if we just fill a need versus really understanding our strengths and how to contribute, then we can end up in a role that consumes the vast majority of our free time and it may be occupying the same space that a connected purpose would have.

Your Marketplace Role Matters

In Genesis 2, after God breathed life into Adam, His very first command was to tend to the garden. In other words, He gave Adam a job. That is why people enjoy work. We are called to enjoy what we do with God. God modeled this for us when He worked extremely hard and passionately for six days on creation, and then He rested in the fruit of His work.

We also know that Paul describes our heavenly occupation and the roles we must play in eternity. When we are in heaven, we will be given a role to play to be part of the symbiotic oneness with God. We will be called to enjoy that role. In Ephesians 1, Paul describes how Jesus was raised up beyond all the roles, titles, professions of authority, and was given the highest place. Then, in Ephesians 2, Paul says we are already seated there with Him in that kind of authority, which means that here on Earth, we are supposed to wield that authority with humility and joy. There is nothing anyone can give us that is higher than what Jesus already gave us when it comes to rank, title, or position. We can serve in the lowest position on Earth and it does not matter because we have been given the highest position in heaven for eternity.

What we do here on Earth for work is extremely important, but even more important is the nature in which we do it. The way we wield our love is our authority and a dress rehearsal for heaven. The picture we have in Revelation 19 is so beautiful. It shows the bride making herself ready. The preparation described is not about external beauty, although we can tell by John's reaction that the bride is beautiful. Instead, this passage is about her being able to fully work with Christ. She is His perfect counterpart. She is His joy set before Him because she knows how to be a true partner.

When God uses us to manifest the Kingdom in our career, we get a glimpse of our favor and significance in His eyes. And when we mature in our ability to relate to God and partner to Him, we begin to see the fruit and blessing of our role as the bride of Christ played out in our everyday lives.

Stepping into Your Marketplace Assignment Requires Humility

Let's look at Solomon and think about how he became the greatest and richest ruler of all time. First, in 1 Kings 3:7-14 (NIV), Solomon admitted his weakness and asked for help and an understanding heart from the Lord. The scripture says this:

> "Lord my God, you have made your servant king in place of my father David. But I am only a little child and do not know how to carry out my duties. Your servant is here among the people you have chosen, a great people, too numerous to count or number. So, Lord, give your servant a discerning heart to govern your people and to distinguish between right and wrong. For who is able to govern this great people of yours?"
>
> The Lord was pleased that Solomon had asked for this. So God said to him, "Since you have asked for this and not for long life or wealth for yourself, nor have asked for the death of your enemies but for discernment in

administering justice, I will do what you have asked. I will give you a wise and discerning heart, so that there will never have been anyone like you, nor will there ever be. Moreover, I will give you what you have not asked for—both wealth and honor—so that in your lifetime you will have no equal among kings. And if you walk in obedience to me and keep my decrees and commands as David your father did, I will give you a long life."

Now, isn't it just like God, when we come to Him in weakness as Solomon did, that God not only answers that but also one-ups it? He says, "Moreover, I will give you what you have not asked for—both wealth and honor—so that in your lifetime you will have no equal among kings."

What an upgrade! God had it in His heart to do way beyond what Solomon could imagine, just like He does for all of us. Solomon used the action and heart of humility in the beginning of his reign as he set up not only himself but also Israel for this vital relationship with the Lord.

As we look at hearing God speak about our role in the marketplace—and in some cases, the church—it starts with the same humble heart and childlike nature that Solomon had. We must be comfortable in our own skin and willing not only to ask God for help but to be humble in our approach to others as well.

When we build our teams or pursue our careers, we need the humility to build with people who are smarter than us so that we can rely on their wisdom and knowledge for the common good of the project, the organization, the role, or the service that we're providing. God loves a humble heart; it is the currency of hearing His voice and understanding the work He has called you to do.

Your Vocation Is Your Assignment from God

So, in that vein, how do we build the spiritual confidence to see our career and our day-to-day job as holy? How do we change our perspective to see that we are assigned to our work by God and it is an act of service and worship to Him? This can be especially difficult when the work we do may not feel like what we dreamed of or imagined for our lives.

Developing our purpose is one of the main themes about which Christian leaders have written books and crafted sermons for ages. Followed, of course, by fulfilling the great commission of getting people saved. But what would happen if that were already fulfilled? What would the world look like if we knew our purpose and everyone was already saved? If we reflect back on the Garden, we see man and woman working in relationship with God, cultivating creation. Before salvation was necessary, there was work. Work does not go away. There are eternal appointments and roles set aside for us. You were made to work, and you have a role to serve. One body, many parts.

Throughout biblical culture, there didn't exist a time when people only did vocational ministry, unless they were a priest or one of the disciples in the New Testament. Even the schools of prophets Samuel initiated were only offered to men of good standing in the community as a career person or business owner. Paul had a tent-making business alongside his ministry as well, and we know that many of the people who were saved in the New Testament had roles in society through government and business. Mary and Martha, along with Lazarus, were believed by most Christian theologians to be very wealthy and influential in their community.

When Christ chose His disciples, He did not pick graduates of the Jewish vocational theology school. He picked people who were immersed in the world's culture and marketplace and willing to learn, shift, and adjust. How crazy is it that He says to the two fishermen, "Follow me," and then walks away? Imagine their conversation afterward: "What did he say?" "He said, 'Follow me.'" "Who is he?" "I don't know. Let's follow him and find out."

What if we followed Christ into the marketplace with the same faith and knowing as the disciples? What if we could hear God clearly not just for our personal needs but also for the greater purposes He has for us on this earth? Fulfilling your assignment, your God-given purpose, is how you demonstrate what Christ looks like to people who would never have the opportunity to see Him if they didn't see you.

By pursuing your career in the marketplace, you are furthering God's purpose to restore all things, to love the entire world, and to bring humanity into relationship with Him.

ACTIVATION

1. Do you feel utilized within the church? How?
2. Do you see any areas where you can serve more, or less, or where your role needs to shift?
3. How do you see yourself doing the work of restoration within your marketplace assignment?
4. Spend time asking God how He sees your marketplace role and the value of your work.

CHAPTER 3

Influence

God wants more than anything else to propel you into your assignment—that thing that you were created for where you fit like a key in a lock.

David Yarnes

The landscape of modern Christianity is being empowered with fresh ideas, ingenuity, and reformation. New voices are emerging to give courage and boldness to engage culture and people with our faith. Even more than that, God has positioned Christians in places of influence and authority, giving us hope and new prototypes for what it means to demonstrate the Kingdom of God here on Earth.

The possibilities with God in the marketplace are endless, far beyond the church's commonly communicated expectations of "get everyone saved" and "love each other." God wants to bring marketplace innovation to meet the growing needs of a diverse world, to better our lives, and to build thriving economies.

Our responsibility to serve in every sector is the foundation of the Kingdom. What if people were shown the face of God through our servitude, innovation, growth, excellence, care, and provision? This is the real-world transformation that God originally intended.

This is not a church-centric move of God. He is not only speaking to cultural leaders in every area of life. He is speaking to each one of us about our call to serve and love within the marketplace. He is placing us in positions of influence—whether influence over an entire organization or industry or influence with a single co-worker—so that we can bring life and light to those around us. He is giving us influence so that we can serve the world.

We are seeing this played out through the most public examples in history. Hollywood industry executive Mark Burnett and his wife, Roma Downey, produce many faith-based shows on top of producing some of the most well-known reality TV shows of the past decade. In an interview with a Christian magazine, Mark said, "People assume that Hollywood lacks faith, which I hope is not the case. When I spoke at Catalyst West a year ago, I was sharing about the Bible and I remember people coming up to me and saying, 'That's so cool. The guy who makes *Survivor* and *The Voice* is a Christian.' If you think about it, some of the greatest written word and visual art in history were made by Christians."[1]

NBA star Stephen Curry regularly discusses the importance of his faith both on and off the basketball court. Internationally acclaimed fashion designer Nancy Vuu left her career in finance when she heard God tell her to pursue fashion instead. Today, God has positioned her to be a voice in an industry where people are starving for love and identity. Dr. Jordan Rubin, who started Garden of Life Nutrition company and Ancient Nutrition, works with business partner Josh Axe to help educate

1   https://www.risenmagazine.com/faith-hollywood-mark-burnett-roma-downey/

the world on health, nutritional science, and regenerative agriculture. We could go on and on. It only takes a moment to identify influencers in various industries that are bringing reformation and transformation. Their influence is across the board, deep and wide, in areas of technology, environment, sports, service, government, education, and countless other areas.

It may seem that those who reach these heights of influence are just a small remnant—the few who make it in their industry or gain enough favor. But when a leader emerges from the ranks into a spotlight of hope and influence, it should give us the perspective that all things are possible.

Once the church sees what it looks like to follow God into the marketplace, others will grab hold of their own hope and step into an accelerated journey. Before long, we will witness a full-scale movement of Christians understanding why God put them in a place of influence and how to walk with God to see His will accomplished in that place. In every sector of society, the incorporation of God's wisdom in the workplace will continue to confound the wise and bring positive solutions in a marketplace that is so desperate for them.

Relationship Over Agenda

We have both consulted many individuals and corporations regarding the voice of God and His desire to communicate with us about every aspect of our lives. And we have come to a similar conclusion through our experience. Christians who are thriving and have that "it" factor in business have one common denominator: they trust their own ability to hear from God and know that life is about connection before it is about task.

Most books that are written about hearing God's voice for the marketplace are all about workplace evangelism, which we love—in the right context. But before God speaks to us about the work we do or the people we are called to reach, His goal is that we would know Him.

He wants us to build His culture in our lives and workplaces, and this alone can speak a thousand words to the people who work with us or for us.

> We think because someone has called us in for business that it is our direct goal to evangelize them. We are trying to answer questions no one is asking. (Bill Johnson)

One day, a young man who graduated from a ministry program came to talk to Bob. He wanted to set up a time to come to Bob's company and pray for the employees to introduce them to Jesus. This young man did not have any connection to, or experience with, the business, and Bob could not imagine what it would look like to bring him into a place where he had no relationship with the people and where the employees had no context for him. It felt unsafe and unloving. Bob knew that the simple act of bringing in a stranger with an agenda would tear down what he had been building with God. It would destroy years of equity that he had with his team, many of whom were not believers. Bob told the young man, "No, thank you, but if you want a job and to build community with them and to share out of the safety of relationship, then I can hire you."

This idea was countercultural to the young man. He thought that Bob was insane for not allowing God into the business through ministry, and he could not understand or honor that Bob was already hearing from God and helping his employees see who God was every day by how he ran the company. The young man went to his church leader, who is a friend of Bob's, in order to "report" him. The church leader, however, was mature enough to see that the young man's agenda was very narrow-minded.

This is a real example of what it looks like when we put our agenda above God's desire to simply love. Yet, what does it look like when we choose to use our influence to demonstrate a different way of doing things? How are people impacted when we change the culture around us instead of trying to convince others to practice our theology?

Let's consider Solomon for a moment. He heard God's voice and shared God's mind and wisdom to lead and develop his kingdom. He was not trying to "Hebrewfy" all the other kingdoms; he was trying to steward the work and words of God. He simply became a living representation of God's wisdom and presence through the way he governed, built, judged, and worshiped. As he lived his life, people from all over came to see what he had built. He did not have to directly do outreach; people saw the God of Israel because of the way the kingdom was built and managed.

When the Queen of Sheba, the richest and most powerful woman of her day, came to see Solomon, she declared that Solomon's god was the true God.

> The report I heard in my own country about your achievements and your wisdom is true. But I did not believe these things until I came and saw with my own eyes. Indeed, not even half was told me; in wisdom and wealth you have far exceeded the report I heard. How happy your people must be! How happy your officials, who continually stand before you and hear your wisdom! Praise be to the Lord your God, who has delighted in you and placed you on the throne of Israel. Because

of the Lord's eternal love for Israel, he has made you
king to maintain justice and righteousness. (1 Kings
10:6-9, NIV)

She had a revelation of who God is because of how Solomon built
the kingdom in the natural and stewarded God's words. He heard God
and there was proof that God not only had something to say but also to
build that affected the world.

This removes the need for performance and the agenda-based evangelism we have come to encourage believers to practice. You were not
put in your job or in a place of influence simply to invite someone to
church or preach the gospel on your lunch break. You were called to
your position, whatever it may be, to serve and demonstrate God's love
to those around you in very practical ways.

Examples of Kingdom Influence

When our focus is on prophetic evangelism in the workplace, it can be
quite disruptive and even cause setbacks for us and those with whom
we work (or those who work for us). Evangelism becomes our agenda
and central theme when the real theme in everything that we do is to
simply walk with God.

We see many examples of this in the Bible but most specifically in
the stories of Joseph in Egypt, Daniel in Babylon, and Esther in Persia.
All three of them were some of the highest-ranking individuals in their
generation who changed the lives of everyone around them simply by
stepping into a place of servitude, walking with God, and doing what
they heard Him say to do.

When Joseph was young, God gave him a dream that Joseph thought
was about him personally. In the dream, he was exalted by his brothers.

In reality, the dream was about how God wanted to sustain Israel through a famine by putting Joseph in a position of influence in order to protect Israel's future. Joseph didn't interpret the dream correctly, and his brothers got jealous and sold him into slavery.

His journey didn't end there, however. In every position Joseph found himself, he chose to serve God and those around him. Despite the trials he faced, God had a plan to position Joseph exactly where he was needed to have the most influence. When the famine arrived and Joseph's brothers came before him, just like his initial dream, Joseph was able to demonstrate God's heart for restoration. He forgave his brothers and his family and restored life and hope to his nation.

For every problem that we face, God already has a plan and a solution in place. He loves humanity and He loves inviting us to partner with Him to bring solutions through divine ingenuity, true leadership, revelation, advice, wisdom, and counsel. God is looking at the issues on the earth right now and is already planning for the world's good. He did so by raising up a Son, but He's also raising up people with a spirit like Joseph to come and influence the world's problems by walking with Him and hearing His voice.

Daniel is another example of what it looks like when Kingdom people lead with God's heart and mind. At the time of his influence, Daniel and the people of Israel were in exile in Babylon. They did not have any influence at all. Daniel and his three friends, however, were set apart and trained by the Babylonians. God gave them not only favor but also a spirit of excellence, knowledge and wisdom, revelation, and divine intelligence in the midst of a Babylonian system that conflicted with their own Jewish traditions.

When Daniel volunteered to interpret the king's dream, a task that none of the king's magicians could accomplish, Daniel and his friends were put in positions of influence. To the other Israelites, it likely appeared that Daniel and the others had sold out to a corrupt and evil government. Why else would they be okay serving a demonic system?

Daniel and his friends, however, were unwavering in their commitment to God. Even in the midst of those demonic systems, they were able to thrive. They were able to bless Babylon for the sake of their people through the reign of multiple rulers. They refused to worship anyone except God, and they listened to God's leading in their service to the Babylonian kings.

We see this same mindset all the time when people today are sent into positions that are almost confusing: influence in the entertainment industry, sports, politics, or areas where it looks like you have to sell your soul to the devil in order to gain any influence. God is sending people into those areas who have a Daniel heart. They're not compromising.

In fact, just like in the story of Daniel, it's actually for the good of all of us that they're in those places of influence. It's for the good of the whole Kingdom, but it's also for the good of what God intended in that industry. God had an original plan for every industry that doesn't include corruption or power struggles. Even if our position only has influence over a small fraction of that industry, when it's seen, it helps to rewire people's thoughts and opinions about that industry's purpose. Whether it is music, video games, TV, or politics, when a righteous person is standing in that area, it influences people far more than any sin or darkness.

Esther, our final example of Kingdom influence, was a woman of no influence. She was an orphan raised by her cousin, Mordecai, in an exiled country with no hopes for herself or her nation. The Jews were in exile under the rule of King Xerxes, whose empire was established as the first superpower in history. The Persian empire covered three million square miles and spanned over three continents: Asia, Europe, and Africa. How would a simple Jewish orphan girl change the course of the Jewish nation?

Xerxes's reputation was one to be feared. At the end of a seven-day feast with other princes and nobles, he called for his Queen Vashti to present herself before his guests. This request sounds simple but was one that could easily put Vashti into harm's way as she would be paraded in front of a drunken crowd. Her refusal cost her the crown and led to her exile from the king's presence. Through this act, we also see that women in this society were severely marginalized.

When the queen lost her position, beautiful young virgins were sought from this vast empire to be prepared to meet the king. Among these was the exceptional Esther. What might she be facing? Relational separation from the only family member she had ever known. Loss of the joy of a Jewish marriage and children once her virginity was taken by the king. Fear for her safety and well-being as she witnessed Vashti's exile for standing up for her dignity.

How do we navigate risks when they can take such extraordinary tolls on our lives?

Esther's deep relationship with Mordecai prepared her in ways to seek beyond herself for answers. One of her foundational gifts was relational trust. Bringing this with her to the king's harem, her first step of favor was found in the eunuch Hegai. He not only made sure her outward beauty was magnificent, but he also gave her his greatest wisdom: "Don't go highly adorned into the king's presence. Come as yourself." Her influence grew through her humility and ability to gather wisdom from others. After twelve months of preparation, Esther was brought to the king and then elevated to a place of influence because of her natural beauty, her character, and her personality.

It would seem that as she was crowned queen, her life moved into its greatest position of influence; however, she held a secret. Among the 30 million people in the Persian empire, Xerxes didn't know that the queen he had chosen was a Jewess. In the midst of her time in the palace, an order was issued to destroy all of her people. Mordecai convinced her, "What if you're in a position that's for all of us? What if God used your beauty or your skill or your talent to put you here and there's a reason for it?"

Esther's fear was palpable. Xerxes had exiled Vashti, and if Esther presented herself to the king unbidden, the sentence was death unless he extended his scepter. Would the embarrassment he experienced because of Vashti cause him to reject Esther? Mordecai reminded her of her influence: "If you die, you die. If we're killed, you won't escape. What if you die for the sake of God's purpose being revealed through people who are going to be set free?"

Esther went from having no family other than her cousin to realizing she was called to be the mother of Israel. She was the person who God raised up to that position in order to save her people. One thing that stands out is the fact that Esther did not choose that position; she hated it. She had a choice when she was drafted into the king's harem: to become a victim or to powerfully walk in the confidence of God's plan for her life.

From this moment, Esther was transformed into a woman of extraordinary wisdom and courage. She called on the people of Israel to fast for three days. She went from listening to Mordecai to finding her own answers from God. Strategies came to her that would not only honor the king but also expose the true enemy. As she grew in her own trust, favor multiplied. Multiple times she went before the king, unbidden, risking her life. Through her choices, Xerxes ended up sending a decree not only for the people of Israel to not be annihilated but also to be able to have weapons and defend themselves. This decree went out in different languages to 127 different provinces, possible only through the edict of the king. Without Esther overcoming her fear and walking in precise obedience, the nation of Israel would not survive today.

She had not chosen this position of influence, but she chose the beauty of relationships and extraordinary obedience at the risk of her life.

There are many of us who find ourselves in positions that we wouldn't have chosen. We may think, *This is not what my college degree is for. This is not the life or role that I imagined for myself.* But what if we are in that position for a much bigger purpose? What if God sent us to be positioned for influence?

God wants to raise up people who hear His voice and know how to influence the world around them with the Kingdom that is within them. What if Esther, Daniel, and Joseph hadn't been positioned for influence? Because they were positioned rightly, however, they changed the course of history. That is what happens when we come into connection with what God has created us for and who He has assigned us to serve and love.

"For we are God's handiwork, created in Christ Jesus to do good works, which God prepared in advance for us to do" (Ephesians 2:10, NIV). Being positioned to influence is not about us. It's all about Him resourcing us with our calling so we can help give Jesus His inheritance.

Influence and Generational Blessing

God loves using His people to bring transformation to the world. We see this so clearly in His original design and how it is still working among the people He called His own. There are tangible milestones visible through the Jewish people today that prove how God's promises throughout history form an astounding miracle that demonstrates to the world who God is and what He is capable of.

When you read scriptures about the Hebrews in the Old Testament, you see God's promises that they will be a people who don't just survive but who will flourish. "But remember the Lord your God, for it is he who gives you the ability to produce wealth, and so confirms his covenant, which he swore to your ancestors, as it is today" (Deuteronomy 8:18, NIV).

When we look at those same promises today, we see a picture of miraculous provision and a people who, against all odds, survived almost being destroyed more than any other group in history. Not only that, they have found unique ways to create wealth and influence that are noticed by almost every major industry in the world.

As of today, the global Jewish population is approximately 0.2 percent of the total populace—some fourteen million people. Yet, in *Vanity Fair*'s 2010 list of the hundred most powerful people in the world, fifty-one were Jewish.[2] Ten of the fifty people on that year's *Forbes* annual billionaires list were also Jewish. Of over 900 individuals who have received a Nobel prize since 1901, at least 20 percent are Jewish.

Forbes once listed that in the top twenty industries in the world, twenty to eighty of the top positions were held by Jewish people. This includes banking and finance, medical industries, and the entertainment industry.

We see this place of influence and wealth as a prototype for how God, who has never changed, wants to bless and use us as well. His promises never fail and are increasing with each generation, seemingly culminating in ours.

The incredible generational promises and blessings that God bestowed on the Israelites also show us that even if we look like we only have a small presence, we have a huge impact in the areas God is calling

2   https://www.jpost.com/Jewish-World/Jewish-Features/Worlds-50-most-influential-Jews-176071

or assigning us to. We can be a David in a Goliath situation and we have both a biblical and modern-day precedent for what that looks like. This does not mean we will have dominion everywhere before Jesus returns, but we will be connected to who God is in our generation and profoundly impact those He loves.

You Have Everything You Need

There has been somewhat of a defeatist mentality in many church circles when it comes to stepping into places of influence in the marketplace. We tend to think that we must wait for something profound to happen before we can really do what we are called to do. We are waiting for resources, relationships, connections, for heaven to be more visible on the earth.

The beauty of walking in the gifts of 1 Corinthians 13, however, is that we have continual access to revelation, discernment, words of wisdom, words of knowledge, and prophecy. And when you walk with the Spirit and carry the mind of Christ, you see the world with eyes of faith and our current age as a divine set-up for God's glory to be revealed, even in the midst of very thick darkness. When you see with His eyes, you have no excuse but to see the restoration of all things that Jesus proclaimed.

Practically, we are already being resourced for one of the greatest assignments to see a whole generation touched by the gospel and Spirit. Proverbs 13:22 says, "And the wealth of the sinner is stored up for [the hands of] the righteous" (AMP). We are set up for a power shift that is worldwide if we allow God to direct our love, give us revelation and unity, and organize our beliefs.

We have heard preachers our whole lives who spoke about a great wealth transfer from the wicked to the righteous based on scriptures just like that verse in Proverbs. The thing is, Christians are already the wealthiest people group in the world.[3] We hold 55 percent of the world's wealth. Over half of the world's billionaires claim Christianity as their faith.[4] The problem is that there is a disconnect between holding that wealth and using it for what God intended. When we choose to walk with God and pursue His heart for our lives and the world around us, we begin to see those resources creating Kingdom transformation across the globe.

You can (and probably already do) hear from God in powerful ways that impact the world around you. Not only that, but you have access to the resources of heaven to accomplish all that God has planned for you. God is assigning you to your career and appointing you to make a difference. He has enabled you to hear from Him to create and steward great resources for His purpose. This should bring you *huge* hope!

Identifying Your Marketplace Influence

Part of stepping into Kingdom influence in the marketplace is understanding your current role and what God has called you to. Throughout our work with people both in and out of the church, we have distinguished four key roles that people are called to within the marketplace. You may have experienced one or all of these roles or find that you are fulfilling several at once. Different seasons and careers will also shift you into different roles. These are not finite but are created to help you identify your current position for marketplace influence.

---

3   https://economictimes.indiatimes.com/news/company/corporate-trends/
     christians-hold-largest-percentage-of-global-wealth-report/articleshow/45886471.
     cms?from=mdr
4   http://sundayadelajablog.com/worlds-richest-christians-including-nigerias-
     billionaire-baroness-folorunsho-alakija/

1. Carrying Culture

   Culture is the composite of behavior evaluated in several areas of life. In the marketplace, there is the invitation to adapt to the prevailing culture of an organization or industry or bring our own. Our role in the marketplace is to bring a culture of love and not fear, as well as Kingdom core values such as honor, liberty, and excellence, to name a few. Culture starts from within and is walked out in every conversation and action we take. Sally, for example, goes to work at her accounting business and brings Kingdom to work by hearing God and implementing great ideas for her team, building a culture of excellence and innovation.

2. Stewarding Resources

   One primary role in the marketplace is stewarding great resources. This, of course, refers to the accumulation, distribution, and the legacy of wealth. Marketplace people are called to build up and create resources to shape lives and change the world. Resources refer to things beyond money, as well, to include anything that can be stewarded: assets, skills, time, and relationships. Whether we are working with tangible or intangible resources, our role as stewards is to bring maximum returns.

3. Service

   "The greatest among you will be the one who always serves others from the heart" (Matthew 23:11, TPT). We are called to serve the needs of society. Once we realize and practice the role of servanthood, all of our relationships will begin to change for the better. A true display of humility is the secret to customer service, vendor relations, employee retention, and promotion. All business is about relationships, and in those relationships our reward is to meet the needs of others.

4. Hearing God for Solutions

As marketplace leaders, we have a mandate from heaven to listen to what God is doing in our lives and industry and to incorporate His heart and mind in all that we do. For example, say that John asks for a creative solution for a problem that his boss is having with a client. He hears from God, gives his boss the suggestion (without telling him God gave it to him), and the solution solves the problem and increases business.

We have made the church the focal point for hearing from God, but God is the creator of all things. Wherever we go, He is there also (see Isaiah 41:10). He is not just in a church building on a Sunday; He is the Church, and we are His body as we go about our lives and share the love of Christ "to the ends of the earth" (Acts 1:8). Our role in the marketplace is to hear God and bring supernatural and natural solutions, business plans, inventions, divine strategy in corporate meetings, and even personal solutions for co-workers and employees. We can hear God for our business or industry problems and opportunities.

For the most part, everyone has a job and works for a living. Even if our role is not financially motivated or involves caring for our loved ones or our household, we all have a job to fulfill, a place of influence. Understanding our current role in the marketplace is vital to knowing how to live out the full potential of and purpose for our lives. We may be a manager and oversee others or work for someone else. Regardless, our ability to invite God into our role and partner with what He is doing is not a matter of rank or position. He wants to partner with us, help us, and build with us!

The work you are doing right now is an important part of your life and your role in the world. It may not be your favorite job, your most desired job, or even your dream job, but you are there right now for a reason, and God has a plan for you. He wants to partner with you in every season in whatever position of authority or influence you may have. What are some areas of influence you can see yourself in right now? What is your David and Goliath situation where you need big answers for big pressing problems? God wants to help you!

ACTIVATION

1. Of the four roles that we identify in this chapter, which one do you most relate to in this season of your life?
2. How do you feel God is calling you to walk out your marketplace role?
3. List several ways that you can serve, support, or bring practical solutions to your workplace without mentioning your faith.
4. What is one area where you need godly wisdom to solve a practical obstacle? Spend time talking to God about His solutions.

CHAPTER 4

Process

Success is remaining faithful to the process God has laid out for you.

Andy Stanley

Susan was finishing up her master's in education in the Midwest. She wanted to reform the education system and, in her late thirties, was gearing up for the long haul in education. But then she was at a church meeting and heard God in a way she knew was undeniable: "You are called to be an actress and minister in the entertainment industry in Los Angeles." She was floored. She did not want this; she had never even taken an acting class. It was completely different from what she had chosen her whole life. She did not understand, but she had told God He could have her life, so she obeyed.

She moved out to California and used her savings to go to acting school. After her money started to run out, she was about to become a substitute teacher while she pursued her craft, but she decided to first get prayer. She approached Shawn at a church service, asking for ministry. Shawn was prompted by the Holy Spirit to say something he had never said before or since: "Are you sure you are supposed to be a substitute teacher? Maybe there is a job that would help you in your new career of acting."

She did not like that answer, but they prayed together anyway. "God, show Susan if there is a job You want her to have that would be good for her career." She said, "Shoot!" and looked almost angry. "What?" Shawn asked.

"I saw myself in a Starbucks barista outfit. This is terrible!" Shawn immediately knew why it was terrible. To be a barista is an awesome dream, but it was not her dream. Not only that, but in the entertainment industry, it's the day job many entertainers resort to in order to support their dream. She could make three times the amount of money as a substitute teacher, but she clearly felt the prompting of God to pursue a job as a barista.

"What if you are going to be around people who God is sending you to love and connect to and even minister to? What if they are going to help you as well?" Shawn asked.

"My best friend back home oversees education in the entire state," she responded. "My other best friend is a principal of an amazing school. I am going to be the woman who left her master's degree to serve coffee. Why is my process so different? Why is God demoting me?"

Shawn knew her friends and recognized that they were not necessarily Christians with a Kingdom agenda. They were great people; their goals were simply not Kingdom focused. "Your friends are not trying to be influencers for Jesus to change the world, so their process is going to be very straight and narrow," Shawn explained. "You, however, have not given Jesus your life hypothetically but realistically, and He is leading you through a process you would have never chosen—but to get to a result you could never manufacture by your own choices. I think you need to trust Him."

She agreed and said, "I will apply at one coffee place and if it's God, I will get the job!" This was in 2009 when there was still some measure of recession in L.A. and the coffee shop that she applied to had hundreds of applications that month for only a couple positions. Who got one of them? Susan. She knew it was God because she had absolutely no experience as a barista.

After working there for six months, she had become the den mom for all the musicians and actors who worked with her. They were not Christians and she had become a voice to their dreams and encouragement to their journey and pain. They all loved her so much. Then one of them got a breakthrough! She got a role on a new show and had to quit her job at the coffee shop in order to pursue it. Every one of the employees felt like her breakthrough brought each of them one step closer to fulfilling their dreams.

When this young woman went to do the table reads the first day, she discovered that one of the other actresses was off the show due to an emergency surgery. The director and producer were at a loss. The young actress heard them talking about it and she had read the character and knew it was right for Susan. The character was an older sister who was matriarchal and nurturing and funny. The young actress risked sounding out of line and asked the director and producer if Susan could come audition. They were so hopeful that they let Susan come straight into the table read the next day. They loved her. She never had an official audition; she simply stepped right into the role.

Now, all these years later, Susan has been cast on one series after another. Although she is not widely known, she has loved on hundreds of people in the industry using this career that God invited her into in order to change the world.

Your Process Will Look Different

As Christians who want our careers to be inspired by God, we must first recognize the importance of our spiritual connection with Him. Christian principles and values will not carry us through life. Our ongoing walk with God—our relationship with Him—is the only thing that will sustain our pursuit of our calling or Kingdom purpose.

Just like Adam was created to work in the Garden and rule over creation, so too there are things God has wired you to do. Ephesians 2:10 (NIV) explains, "For we are God's handiwork, created in Christ Jesus to do good works, which God prepared in advance for us to do."

When we consider our job, career, startup, or business endeavor, are we viewing it as the "good works" that God prepared for us? Is our vocation a holy, God-ordained pursuit? When we begin to view our work through the lens of Kingdom purpose, we quickly realize that our process *must* look different from that of those around us. We cannot get from point A to point Z without God. Our process is not going to look the way we might choose for it to look, and the path may not be direct, but it will be God's process and we get to choose to walk it out with Him by our side.

To pursue spiritual fruit in our natural career, our process needs to be led spiritually. If we give God the leadership of our business, career, or path, we are giving up some of our rights to do things our way. We will not be able to compare ourselves to others who are pursuing the same thing or else we will become discouraged. If we are focused on and treasuring the things we are giving up (our freedom, our security, maybe relationships or where we live), then we will most likely not make it through the process with Him.

We love what the writer of Hebrews said about those who are examples of faith:

And if their hearts were still remembering what they left behind, they would have found an opportunity to go back. But they could not turn back for their hearts were fixed on what was far greater, that is, the heavenly realm! (Hebrews 11:15-16, TPT)

When we choose God's process, it is more than likely that we will not have the same life journey, education, or experience as others who are going after the same career. God knows how to strip us of our carnal natures: pride, self-reliance, lack of emotional intelligence, lack of empathy. He puts us in positions that cause the best in us to come out and the worst in us to be stripped away.

Bob started his business at age eighteen with a VW bug kitted with surf racks to carry ladders. He took his fledgling painting business seriously. He loved painting and enjoyed the process of learning how to grow the business. As the years passed, he began to employ other people. Business was good, but progress was slow.

At the time, many of his friends were in full-time ministry, and sometimes he felt marginalized by their quick access to great spiritual opportunity when his life felt like it was happening more slowly. Despite his feeling of isolation from the spiritual opportunities and world of his friends, Bob continued to be faithful in his business and the path God had placed him on.

Eventually, because of his level of responsibility and dependability, he became an elder in his church at a young age. This role exposed him to many incredible church leaders and ministers. People would ask him, "Why aren't you a pastor?" And he would say, "Because I am a painter."

The truth is, Bob began to see that as someone who employs other people, he had a sacred role in many areas of his employees' lives. He was responsible for creating jobs, culture, safety, and quality of life. He was pastoring, in many ways, by caring for the livelihood and mental, emotional, and physical health of his staff.

He learned to love every job that came his way, the little and the big jobs, because in each of them he was partnering with God. Over the years, Bob began to identify that what he really loved was the transformation: old walls becoming new walls; old color being replaced with fresh, new colors. He also loved watching employees, vendors, and customers transformed by their interaction with a company operating with honor, and letting its yes be yes, and its no be no (see Matthew 5:37). Fast-forward forty-two years and he is still in the transformation business. But now he is seeing transformation in corporate culture, employees, and entire organizations as he consults with other businesses.

Bob's process was entirely different from that of his closest friends and colleagues. He wanted to have Kingdom fruit—not just financial fruit or notoriety—in his career, so he followed what he felt was right based on what he heard God saying. For forty years he pursued God's calling to the marketplace. He built a business (with ups and downs) and in his spare time supported ministers, itinerants, and his local church. The marketplace, however, was always his vocation. Then, somewhere around 2015, the two roles merged and God began to give Bob a voice in the world of organized Christianity. That hadn't ever been his goal, but God used both the strengths and mistakes Bob had learned throughout his career as a means to consult with Christians, entrepreneurs, and business leaders.

Our process will always look different from the average person because our motivation is different. As Christians, we have a clearly defined biblical parameter in which we build our goals, a parameter that connects everything we do to our relationship with God. Walking out this process is not always easy, but when we choose to partner with God in our careers, we get to bear witness to incredible fruit that we might not otherwise see: the transformation of lives, industries, businesses, and culture.

Be Obedient to His Process

We are all seeking a deeper understanding of our role and place on this earth. Part of hearing God's voice regarding our purpose in the marketplace comes from pressing in and understanding the ways that He is leading us and being obedient to His process. When Joseph was in prison, he could never have imagined that one day he would be the governor of the land. Instead, he chose to recognize God's purposes in his current reality, and his trust and obedience allowed him to thrive and remain hopeful in that place.

While many of us feel like Joseph throughout our processes, wondering where on earth God is leading us, and working hard to trust His process, others will experience more clarity on their journey. And that is okay! We've walked with those who experience the exact trajectory and process that God showed them they would take. That is not the majority, however. For others, lack of clarity is often an invitation from God to dream with Him, to imagine an outcome that we couldn't accomplish on our own.

We are not self-made people. We are in relationship with God, and He is leading us, sometimes into places we wouldn't necessarily choose to go. But even when things don't look the way we think they should, our process is to follow God's voice. Much like Saul (Paul) had to learn how to be led by the directives of God when he was struck blind, we too have to learn to follow God's lead even when we can't see what lies ahead or where the path is meant to lead. This is the reason we often feel like our friends are on a different path—sometimes what appears to be a more direct route to success—like we saw with Susan's process.

God's ways are not our ways. The sooner we understand this truth, the sooner we will learn to recognize God's process in our lives. Not only will it look different from the standard path within the marketplace, but it will also look different from the path of those around us. There is no defined five-step process to success with God. Instead, our lives become a trust fall. As we trust Him and hear His voice, we slowly learn to walk the path He has laid out for us.

As we walk with Him, we learn to see His patterns. We recognize the signposts He has placed for us to see, saying "You are here!" These signposts remind us that we are right smack dab in the middle of His will even when we don't understand where we are. God provides us with spiritual clarity.

Shawn knew a young couple who, one day, felt God say, "I want you to travel the world and show the people in the world what it looks like and give them a love for the beauty of the world." The husband had a career where he could work remotely, but it was still a risk to travel. They decided to be obedient and take that risk. They gave up their apartment and started traveling places, taking beautiful pictures and sharing them on Instagram when Instagram became popular. They started to gain a following and people loved what they were sharing.

Then as they grew, they became sponsored everywhere they went. The hotels would pay them to come because they wanted them as brand ambassadors. They wanted to see their business shared on the couple's Instagram because it was getting so much traffic. Today, the couple have over a million followers on Instagram. This couple knew that God had called them to something significant, and He had blessed it. They also knew it could not be directly reproduced, but they encouraged people all over to listen to God's direction and to obey.

One thing we often hear is people who claim to have heard something from God but who did not do anything with what they heard. In the investment world, we hear people say, "I had the opportunity to invest in Amazon when it was at $18, and I didn't do it. I knew it was going to be big. I knew it in my gut."

God is inviting us into amazing opportunities all the time, but the things that set some people apart are their obedience and perseverance. Even when the process seems unexpected or difficult, they persevere in obedience to God's word, reassessing His call with childlike wonder and an open heart to advance in relationship with God and the world around them.

At one point, Shawn was in full-time ministry, but the type of ministry he was working in was not providing the income he needed. He also didn't feel called to make a career out of that ministry. As he prayed for a few months, he felt like God was opening his heart to non-ministry occupations. This concerned him, however, because he didn't want to do anything he wasn't interested in.

That is often how we think about the opportunities God gives us: we assume they will not be what we want to do. In some ways, we self-protect and do not listen to God because we are afraid to be led by someone else's agenda. In that moment, Shawn had to surrender that fear.

A friend's daughter had recently started a company making video games, with the underlying goal of teaching her sons about business. She wanted to use a business they would be interested in, so she chose video games. She called to ask if Shawn would consult with her before she launched the business. They talked, and after the first phone call, Shawn was hired to consult with her company. It was not his style of game, but he knew the video game industry relatively well and his knowledge was relevant to them. Eventually, Shawn was hired to manage the project, but the owner also had a value for ministry and so she let Shawn split his time between the business and his ministry endeavors.

The company did well, and pretty soon they were working with a

Universal company and it was exciting and lucrative. For years after that, Shawn worked in different aspects of the video game industry alongside his ministry, a path he wouldn't have chosen for himself.

This process, God's process, requires obedience, but it also requires sacrifice. At times, we have to sacrifice our own belief systems in order to step out in faith into a role, career, or task that doesn't make sense. We have to sacrifice the opportunities that feel better than what God is asking us to do. We have to keep our moral compass steady and stay true to our standards, even when those around us are compromising theirs in exchange for success.

It is often in those moments of sacrifice that you can see God's process more clearly. Shawn experienced this when advisers encouraged him to move to Dallas because of a tax incentive. By basing his ministry and business in Texas, he could significantly reduce the state tax burden. Shawn knew, however, that they were meant to be in California. He could see how God's process for his life had firmly planted them to support God's purpose in that state—to be rooted there, even financially. To compromise that would be to shift away from God's leading.

We are accountable to Jesus. We are accountable to the things He is calling us to do, even when the process is unclear, or simply not what we imagined. But He created a blueprint for us to follow:

> Trust in the Lord completely, and do not rely on your own opinions. With all your heart rely on him to guide you, and he will lead you in every decision you make. Become intimate with him in whatever you do, and he will lead you wherever you go. (Proverbs 3:5-6, TPT)

Trust, follow His lead, sacrifice your own opinion, and know that He is guiding you, even when you cannot see the way.

Make Plans with God

Trusting God's process for our lives doesn't negate the value of making a plan. In fact, it is through trust and faith that we choose to lean on the plans that God has prepared for us.

Many years ago, a pastor was referred to Bob because his church was having cash flow issues and having a hard time making payroll and paying its debts. As a consultant, Bob reviewed financial documents, profit and loss statements, spreadsheets, and pro forma forecasting in order to hear God for all a company or ministry had and could have in the future.

After reviewing the documents, Bob met with the pastor and outlined a strategic plan. The pastor looked at him and said, "I don't believe in planning and I think that your plans show that you do not trust God."

Bob sat back in his chair and said, "Well, how is that working out for you?" He then referenced Jeremiah 29:11: "'For I know the plans I have for you,' declares the Lord, 'plans to prosper you and not to harm you, plans to give you hope and a future.'" Even God makes plans, and He is eager to reveal them to us. We have an opportunity to partner with the greatest planner in existence to build a strategic plan for our lives like no other.

This particular pastor chose not to embrace a planning process with God. Sometimes strategy works, sometimes faith works, but we find that both working together is the most powerful combination.

It is impossible to partner with God without faith at work in our decisions. He puts things in front of us not as dangling carrots but as invitations into the impossible. He invites us to pursue things that we couldn't do in our own nature or with our own skill so that when people look at us, they begin to ask questions that lead them back to the statement: "There has to be a God who, if I give my life to Him, will give me a different life back than I could make on my own." You are the proof!

Planning with God combines faith, trust, and strategy and removes things such as stress and anxiety. When you process any major anxiety with God, and partner with His plan and process, the culture around you begins to change.

When we do not have Christ-based goals and plans in our decision making, we are relying on ourselves and our decisions, which can hurt everyone we lead. Each one of our choices is affected by our connection to God. We have a divine tension of standing in faith while planning for the future.

When we bring God into the little stuff, the daily moments, the mundane financial planning and administration, we start to see how His plans for us are far greater than we could imagine. Foundationally, if we bring God into every area of our lives, it will give us a sense of wellbeing, of peace, and can help us make huge decisions. "Whoever can be trusted with very little can also be trusted with much" (Luke 16:10).

Bob once consulted with some young pastors who came to him seeking help with their finances. They needed some help establishing systems, cleaning up their books, and building a strategy to steward their church's finances. When Bob looked through the reports, he saw that they had $600,000 in savings! They had already stewarded their finances well, and Bob was able to encourage their hard work. He helped them establish systems and pull the right reports so that they could better plan for the future and decide how to strategically build on what they already had.

Making plans with God is building strategies that are bathed in prayer. It is getting our house in order so that we can be a blessing to those around us and pass down a spiritual, financial, and emotional inheritance. That is the process and the journey that we are on with God.

Planning and stewarding require faith in the form of obedience to what He has called us to so that we can bring the manifest love of God into practical situations in our everyday lives.

Become Teachable

When you surrender to God and let Him lead you in His process, you must also get into a learning mode. Even if you are an expert in your field, God has full rights to upend your process and place you where you are needed most. For that, you must be teachable.

Shawn and his wife, Cherie, moved into a new home with an acre of land filled with beautiful garden beds that were planted with all the wrong things. Cherie began replanting their property, which needed a complete overhaul. She started to come alive and learn about their specific gardening zone. Her learning took her from landscaping to planting raised-bed gardens, and she became passionate about garden-to-table food and food security.

Poor agricultural practices were (and are) destroying much of our usable soil worldwide. The very first role God gave us is the very thing most Christians have abandoned: tending the land.

Cherie got so passionate, she went on social media and started to share how to garden and prepare garden foods. She named her account "Dream Big Urban Farm" and BuzzFeed picked up some of her videos and she went semi-viral. In the spiritual process of it all, her identity and all the jobs she had ever pursued started to weave together. She had spent a year in culinary school and then interned and worked for years in hospitality at the largest hotel in Vermont, where she was raised, and even got employee of the year for her role in event management. She worked in some well-known restaurants before stepping into ministry and the corporate world.

She had been dreaming with God throughout her adult life, but her opportunities and the roadmap to her destination didn't seem to ever line up. Her activities were eclectic, and they did not paint a clear picture as she followed God's voice from one adventure to another. Until one day the picture became crystal clear.

When the gardening/cooking/influencer piece took off, Cherie started to draw from her experience in different parts of her life and everything synergized. She became like a hungry child and devoured hundreds of hours of farming and gardening classes and YouTube learning. It wasn't for anyone else except her own growth journey. This led her to a very natural change of occupations where she is focusing on making media, entertainment, and social influence for garden-to-table efforts, as well as helping people to connect to their responsibility over the environment. When she started out, she admits that she would have never seen her heart for ministry, the Kingdom, entertainment, food, gardening, and the environment being wrapped up into one role.

In her long journey of Christianity, God was letting her see the road laid out in front of her, and she still has not taken her eyes off of what He is showing her. She approaches everything with childlike curiosity and is continually seeking new understanding of things she has already seemingly mastered.

When we offer our hearts in a teachable way, it takes a measure of frustration out of the journey. We are being led by God, not by our own plans and agenda, and we won't always see what is ahead in the short or long term. Susan lived out this very truth as well. She was pursuing a career as a lifelong learner and educator, but she dropped everything she had worked toward in order to completely start over by learning a new skill as an actress. When we trust God and remain teachable, we enjoy parts of the journey that others just can't wait to get past. We will enjoy the process.

What makes somebody a learner? Are they willing to learn new things through the process of life and relationship? Are they willing to go back and take some classes or get online education if they need it? Are they open to letting their character be reformed in areas that were secure in career paths that felt safe and comfortable but are now vulnerable and new?

Embracing God's process takes some measure of curiosity and childlikeness. When someone really feels like they want to grow, it is because they've regained a childlike wonder, just as Cherie and Susan did. Our minds become like that of a kindergartener whose neurons are firing continually and who is asking a million questions a day.

Learning and becoming teachable, however, isn't just about gaining knowledge but also about applying it. Every day Cherie applies new knowledge to the things she grows or cooks. She then shares it on her social media channels so that she can extend her experiential knowledge to the world.

Some people are naturally adaptable learners, which means they love to learn because they can then produce something with it. Adaptable learning requires change and a willingness to persevere. Our flesh hates any changes that do not have immediate gratification, which is why so many people are learners but do not pursue ways to apply and experience their knowledge and continue learning.

We knew a gardener who could never grow his business past a one-man operation, but he was an incredibly intellectual and academic man. He decided to give this intellectual knowledge away by being a success coach. However, his knowledge had never been proven by his leadership or experience.

He wanted to coach people about wealth and success because he understood the principles. One day, he was asked, "Why would I come to you as a business coach? What do you have to differentiate yourself

from other business coaches? Because your business has never grown."
He felt like he would be good at leading people through coaching principles anyway, but he has not ever been very successful.

His problem was that he was teachable in gaining knowledge but
not in applying it. He cut his learning process short by never learning
from experience. This is where a lot of Christians who are experiencing
a lack of success and contentment live.

Our process must be different. When we approach our lives with
a teachable heart, we open the door for God to place us in positions of
influence and support that we might not have otherwise experienced.
God has a plan and purpose for your life. He has called you into a career
that He created for you and is inviting you to dream, plan, and learn with
Him so that you can step into new realms of influence.

Choosing God's Process

Choosing to partner with God in His process for our lives is one of the
most exciting adventures we will experience. In moments of doubt
or confusion, we love to hold onto these scriptures: Ephesians 3:20;
Jeremiah 29:11; 1 Corinthians 2:9. They remind us that God has huge
plans beyond what we can hope for or imagine or believe for in this lifetime. They are an invitation to live a life that we are not worthy of.

"Plans for a hope and a future" give us great courage. Imagine it: The
Creator of the universe has plans for us! We are heirs to His throne and
therefore have access to everything within His Kingdom. That truth will
change the legacy of your life! That is the kind of opportunity God has
for us as we learn to tune in and listen and obey even when it creates a
process we wouldn't have chosen for ourselves.

ACTIVATION

1. Identify a person in your life who is teachable and whom you admire.
2. What are you currently doing to grow and learn?
3. How do you find or hear God in your daily life?
4. What process did you use to find your career? Where was God in the process?
5. Can you remember when God called you to your initial purpose?

CHAPTER 5

Intuition

Who gives intuition to the heart and instinct to the mind?

Job 38:36, NLT

We were made in God's image, and part of our nature includes the wiring to make powerful choices for our lives. Having the mind of Christ means knowing how to choose things that are the right things for us. Yes, there is also original sin, which is the pattern of fallen man that we are born into. If you have ever been around toddlers, you know it doesn't take much to prove original sin or how selfish humans are. This sinful identity came from us being stripped from partnership and connection with God when Adam and Eve left the garden, and it is compounded by thousands of years of separation.

What a lot of Christians do not consider, however, is that God's original goodness, nature, and wiring were not stripped from man. God created us to be like Him, and although He allowed us to be separated until Jesus, He never short-circuited our wiring to love, to want a healthy life, to see the best in the world around us, and to want freedom. These are all things that we inherently carry, even if sinful patterns get in the way or do not let us realize the fullness of our true nature.

Have you ever seen a businessperson, athlete, or celebrity with massive integrity who is agnostic? Have you encountered people who demonstrate incredible love and compassion but who don't have a relationship with Christ? God never took away the benefit of being made in His image, regardless of our belief systems or even our lifestyles. As a matter of fact, God gave humanity His nature as a free gift and it works with or without a born-again experience. His nature, however, is perfected in us and brought into wholeness and everlasting fruit when it's chosen through a relationship with Jesus.

The Message translation provides a unique perspective on how God's nature is more clearly reflected in us when we choose Christ:

> But what happens when we live God's way? He brings gifts into our lives, much the same way that fruit appears in an orchard—things like affection for others, exuberance about life, serenity. We develop a willingness to stick with things, a sense of compassion in the heart, and a conviction that a basic holiness permeates things and people. We find ourselves involved in loyal commitments, not needing to force our way in life, able to marshal and direct our energies wisely. (Galatians 5:22-23)

Take a moment to reflect on this verse, especially this line: "We develop a willingness to stick with things, a sense of compassion in the heart, and *a conviction that a basic holiness permeates things and people.*"

What a beautiful image of the world and humanity this exposes us to. As Christians, we should look at all the people and things God created as though they can be restored, and as though God is already at work in their lives, in the environment, in government, in all kinds of areas, as though they are already holy because they are made in the image of the Creator.

We see this truth reflected in Genesis 40:8 (NIV) as Joseph was about to interpret dreams of two non-Hebrew men: "Do not interpretations belong to God?" he asked. He believed that God had something to say even to those men. A basic holiness permeates things and people, and God is speaking to His creation.

In the New Testament, we see this when Jesus speaks to the Samaritan woman at the well in John 4. Her race, at the time, was denigrated and even despised by Jewish people to the degree that it was forbidden for Samaritans and Jews to interact. Jesus disregarded that entirely and prophesied over her, explaining God's heart for her. He washed away the division between the people groups and expressed a new reality: that God is in all things and that He is not dividing but seeking those who know His spirit.

The Kingdom of God does not begin with our conversion. It has been woven into the fabric of God's creation but is brought into its intended purpose through believers who walk with God and worship Him. Before we proclaim as evil what God has created, we need to recognize that people are His if they have any time left on this earth. God wired everyone to be a reflection of His glory, including you. That reflection can only be perfected, however, through Jesus.

Instinct and Intuition

Because of this wiring, when we choose to walk with Christ, we have two huge keys that God gave humanity as a leg up in life. We not only get to have fellowship with the Holy Spirit and know the thoughts of God, but we are also wired with intuition and instinct that will help us understand what God is saying. This intuition, or discernment, isn't just about receiving and interpreting prophetic words. It's about trusting what God has put inside of you and operating out of your spiritual, God-given image.

One of the primary virtues of successful marketplace leaders in the Kingdom is that they recognize how to hear God through their instinct and intuition. They do this by learning from their missteps, the moments when they misinterpreted their intuition and instinct. Those who are extremely successful choose not to live in the shame of their mistakes but move on, because they trust the sum of their instinct or intuition—they trust that it is God-given—even when they get it wrong.

Instinct is a natural ability that helps you decide what to do or how to act without thinking: a natural or inherent aptitude, impulse, or capacity (Webster's Dictionary). Instinct is also the ability to behave in a way that has not been learned, which is reflected in ideas such as maternal, financial, or creative instinct.

Intuition, on the other hand, is an ability to understand or know something immediately based on your feelings rather than facts (Webster's Dictionary). It is quick and ready insight that comes without conscious reasoning. When we function from intuition, there is often no clear evidence one way or the other and we simply know something without thinking about it.

The processes that lead us to intuit something are often developed through learning (knowing God, studying His Word and character, hearing His voice) but we utilize them subconsciously. Instinct is, in many ways, hardwired into our personality. Both, however, are from God and perfected in Christ.

Developing Instinct

God has created each one of us with different abilities or instincts for what He has called us to. Just like a caterpillar knows to build a cocoon and that it will somehow transform into something else, there are plans of God inside of us that He reveals to us through instinct. When we follow that instinct, we end up in our correct lane in life.

We hear this a lot in business: "He has good instinct." "Her gut is bar none." "He knew to stay in when everyone else got out." "She was able to follow instinct when the facts said otherwise." This ability to follow instinct is one of the main virtues of game-changing leaders.

Bob has a friend who was a partner at a financial services company, and he had this gut instinct about things. He was in the M&A division and he told Bob, "I just have this gift to be able to look at financial statements and documents of large public companies and have a complete understanding of their financial picture."

Bob watched him put together complex deal after complex deal. His success came not just from hearing God but also from partnering with his God-given instinct. Everyone has the ability to use their instinct from God, but for most of us, this requires work and commitment to learn how to listen to our instinct.

In Malcolm Gladwell's book *The Outliers*, he writes that you need 10,000 hours to be a phenom—10,000 hours to be so freakishly awesome, to be such a standout among your peers, that your first name is enough to tell people who you are: Peyton. Venus. Kobe. Oprah.

Part of the reason why it takes time and experience, even with natural instinct, is that you need a track record and a proving ground. Some people may have a huge win and make a billion dollars by marketing a new app, but can they maintain that success like Zuckerberg or Gates?

Or were they a one-hit wonder because the scope of the success was not partnered to teachability and purpose?

The best place your instinct is developed is in the field God is calling you to tend. Much like the parable of the treasure hidden in the field (see Matthew 13:44), one man has the instinct to sell all he owns and buy up the field. In some ways this parable is counterintuitive. Wouldn't God tell us to tell the original owners that there is a treasure there more valuable than they thought, and they should sell it for more? No, Jesus is talking about the instinct to recognize and develop something that no one else sees. This is part of the way we are wired for relationships, the marketplace, and even social justice issues. We are called to see the treasure in the field while everyone else just sees business as usual.

Within the marketplace, instinct will help you to recognize when you don't have it so that you can hire or bring someone else into your process who does. We have seen companies that fail because the leader did not have the foresight to pivot or change when everything around them was changing. When we know how to operate within our God-given instinct, we will recognize the need for change and will automatically look for someone who carries the solution we need. Lack of instinct, especially in the marketplace, often causes businesses to run aground, forcing entrepreneurs and business leaders to start again from the beginning.

When we embrace good instincts and understand our relationship with God, it brings about a solid marketplace identity. The thing about empowered people is that they attract other empowered people. It's not really opportunity that is king; it is relationship. Opportunity sometimes takes a front seat, but relationships guide the journey so that people with creative ingenuity and good instincts will attract others who want to invest in them, promote them, resource them, etc.

In his book *Good to Great*, Jim Collins and his team of researchers spent five years studying 1,435 companies and the eleven that went from mediocre to outstanding for a sustained period of time. They asked what made those eleven companies stand out above the rest. What was the moment of change that took them from good to great? What they discovered wasn't a moment of miraculous change in each company but a longevity of instinctive and intuitive decisions that the leaders themselves described as "luck":

> Level 5 leaders look out the window to apportion credit
> to factors outside themselves when things go well (and
> if they cannot find a specific person or event to give
> credit to, they credit good luck). At the same time, they
> look in the mirror to apportion responsibility, never
> blaming bad luck when things go poorly. (Jim Collins,
> *Good to Great*)

When we start to recognize instinct as a God-given part of our make-up, it is easy to see God's hand in our marketplace efforts. We begin to understand the promptings of the Holy Spirit and the still small voice in a whole new way, realizing that God cares about the decisions we make for our companies and careers.

Paul Lauer is the head of Motive Marketing, which marketed *The Passion of the Christ*. He and his partners and team had incredible instinct for some of the disruptive ways the entertainment industry could be reached through the church for Mel Gibson's movie to be fully supported as a mainstream film. Paul and Mel and their team ran an incredible outside-of-the-box, day-by-day marketing campaign, and the movie became one of the most viewed movies in history with a financial impact that changed the industry for a somewhat independent film.

Shawn asked Paul why he thought they were able to accomplish this, and they talked about being guided by the Holy Spirit. They felt the inward nudge of God where they could feel what to do next. This is a great example of how God speaks through instinct, an aspect of God's voice that most of the church does not talk about.

Making Decisions with Intuition

According to Businessdictionary.com, intuition is an unconscious thought process that produces rapid, uninterrupted knowledge or solutions. Though it is not analytic in the sense that it does not deliberately look for cause-and-effect (causal) relationships, intuition is not mere guesswork. Instead, it draws on previously acquired experiences and information and directly apprehends a totality. Intuition can be visionary or delusionary, uncannily correct or horrendously wrong in its conclusions.

As we look at how intuition affects Christians in the marketplace (and in other areas), it's important to look at this for what it is. Intuition is the use of a gut feeling to make decisions rather than relying on a more scientific approach using data and other quantitative evidence that is supported by logical, rational decision-making models.

There are many benefits to intuition in decision making, but here are our four favorites:

1. Intuition helps you make decisions faster: When utilizing intuition, making decisions is quick or even instant, instead of waiting on data analysis or scientific or sociological measurement. Intuition is more based on your own personal experience. The data you can research isn't always reliable, and you may feel more secure with the gut feeling, even if it seems to contradict the results suggested by data and the Holy Spirit and wise counselors.

2. Intuition connects decisions to your heart and spirit: Intuition feels more like you are deciding from the heart versus the head. Or, as a Christian, it feels more like you are trying to partner with the Spirit of God through faith instead of just taking status quo for your final authority. At one time, Shawn sat down with a business leader who is part of many wealthy endeavors, and he shared how he had a gift to see patterns in failing companies. He would have his team bring in a hundred companies that were up for sale and were failing but had potential if restructured. He could look through and read and just have a gut feeling about which ones to buy and rebuild and which ones were not worth it.

   He had so much success in this place of intuition and always thought he had an uncanny ability to understand patterns. Then, as he started to develop his relationship with God, he recognized God's wiring in him and began to partner with the Holy Spirit to actually buy and rebuild companies that could affect regional or even national economies if rebuilt correctly.

3. Combining data and intuition often confirms your gut decisions: Intuition is a powerful force within us and one of the main ways a lot of us hear from God. Our wiring and connection to God help us to make great gut decisions. On top of that, when we add getting the research and data we need to help inform these decisions, it often will not conflict with our gut once we've combined the two together.

4. Intuition recognizes times and seasons: Understanding the times and the seasons of life is one of the main

benefits of good intuition. We begin to get excited about
what God wants to do, and no matter what the weath-
erman says, we see a higher report of what is available.

While intuition is similar to instinct, the process of "knowing" is
more connected to our feelings, sometimes sitting in the same place as
our empathy or emotions. Other times, intuition occurs in the driving
places of our minds (remember, we have the mind of Christ). Intuition
often helps us understand what season we are in. It helps us navigate
questions, such as these: Is it time to transition and switch companies
or is it time to practice loyalty to my current company, even if there is
no visual benefit? Or is it a time of explosive growth that I can capitalize
on in my own life?

Intuition helped Solomon know his times and seasons, which he
shared about in Ecclesiastes 3:1-8 (NIV):

> There is a time for everything, and a season for every
> activity under the heavens: a time to be born and a time
> to die, a time to plant and a time to uproot, a time to
> kill and a time to heal, a time to tear down and a time
> to build, a time to weep and a time to laugh, a time to
> mourn and a time to dance, a time to scatter stones and
> a time to gather them, a time to embrace and a time to
> refrain from embracing, a time to search and a time to
> give up, a time to keep and a time to throw away, a time
> to tear and a time to mend, a time to be silent and a time
> to speak, a time to love and a time to hate, a time for war
> and a time for peace.

Intuition helped Bob in his consulting with Bolz Ministries for the past few years. He intuitively knew to encourage the organization to keep building materials and resources, which would increase inventory and decrease cash. He recognized that the ministry would be stepping into a season of resourcing others and that the organization needed to have the base inventory—books, media, podcasts, and other projects—ready for when expansion happened so that people could have a broader way to connect to the message.

Sometimes, when a consultant looks into an organization, it's his or her job to give courage and insight into situations that the consultant has already been through. This is how instinct and intuition work when people are helping others in a business setting. It is a combination of risk management and asking God for solutions, and then partnering with those solutions. As Bob consults with both ministries and marketplaces, his instinct and intuition allow him to see the favor and the destiny and recognize the season they are in.

Part of using intuition to recognize times and season is also putting on our risk manager hat. Risk management, when paired with intuition, helps us weigh the cost of the choices our intuition and instinct are telling us to make. While we, as Christians, often equate risk management with a lack of faith or with unbelief, that is simply not the case. Instead, it can be a healthy part of counting the costs of our intuition. It is a tool that allows us to look at all sides of an issue alongside our intuitive understanding of the times and seasons.

Intuition and Relationships

When we have healthy intuition at work, it helps us to know who our people are—in other words, who is compatible with us and who we should build with. It allows us to create a holistic relationship with others that feels like family and not just an alliance or business partnership.

Many people become unequally yoked in life and business, which is a biblical expression found in 2 Corinthians 6:14. The idea comes from when one ox carries more weight than the other while plowing. You want equally strong oxen in order to efficiently and successfully plow, otherwise an unequal yoke creates problems. One of the reasons why God gives us instinct and intuition from His Spirit is so we can actually know on a deep level who to be yoked with and how to partner with the world that He loves so much.

In Luke 2, we read the stories of Simeon and Anna, who meet Jesus in the temple. They both immediately recognize Jesus as the Messiah; it was instinct and intuition. Anna and Simeon were hardwired to recognize God, and we are as well. That means we can hear God, through our intuition, and recognize Him in those around us. Not only that, but we can also recognize those whose spirit, gifting, or calling is equally yoked to our own.

Five Steps to Develop Instinct and Intuition

Many of us have become too busy or too educated to hear what our instinct and intuition are trying to say. We intellectualize because we are so bombarded with information that we simply cannot hear our gut in the midst of the clutter. Part of developing our relationship with God is to see how He has wired us to connect with Him through instinct and intuition, and learn to hear His voice. It will change our lives so much when we do.

Many major business leaders are hiring intuition coaches now to teach them to listen, and we believe this is valuable. But how much more powerful can our intuition become when we realize that we have the Holy Spirit? One of His names is counselor, coach or teacher, and He loves to use our intuition to connect with us and counsel us. These are five ways to learn how to recognize Holy Spirit intuition in your life:

1. Take time and pause: One of the ways we develop our natural instinct and intuition is to take pauses in our day—especially when we are in a decision-making time—to meditate and be quiet. This means giving ourselves time to pause and check in with the Spirit and listen inwardly to the voice that is processing inside of us. Having regular slow-down times with intentional practices amid fast-paced times is the only way to keep going forward. As Psalm 5:3 says, "In the morning, Lord, you hear my voice; in the morning I lay my requests before you and wait expectantly."

2. Recognize mistakes as a vehicle for learning: We can't camp around our mistakes. Instead, we can ask God to show us how He wants to use them for our good. As we repent for what we need to repent of and allow Him to heal what needs to be healed, we can look for lessons that these mistakes have defined. These are the moments when we do not need to just say, "I would never do that again"; they are the moments we need to ask, "Why did I do that, God? Show me my heart." This creates a teachability where we can pivot from what did not work and trust our gut for what can work in the future.

3. Recognize wins and when things went right: We also need to learn from when we did partner with God, reverse engineering our wins. Does this current moment feel like that time you made a good gut decision? Do you

feel the same presence of mind and heart to make the same decision again? Does it feel familiar? This is one of the main ways we will learn to hear from God. But it requires slowing down, pausing, and evaluating.

4.   Detach emotionally and look from many angles: In the midst of a decision, pause and try to detach from all the potential outcomes so that you can listen to intuition more clearly. Sometimes (like applying for a job or turning in a script) we are so obsessed with the outcome that we cannot truly hear. This does not mean detaching from faith, but allowing ourselves to see what we are looking at from many sides with many outcomes can help us to hear more clearly.

5.   Listen to the people God has put in your life: For us, even when we are fairly sure we know which direction to go in business or ministry, we still include our teams. We sit down with them because our teams are familiar and intimate not only with us but also with the business. As we begin to lay out an idea, we invite them to offer their own intuitive input and direction. Proverbs 15:22 (NIV) says, "Plans fail for lack of counsel, but with many advisers they succeed."

Wired to Make Good Decisions

Most of us use checklists to help decide which opportunities to take. The lists can have things on it like these: Does this fit into my life right now? Is this where my life is going? Does this match my perception of my calling? Does this create the right financial picture? Am I skilled at this? These are all our normal questions, but we need to add the big one:

What does God say about this? Then we need to listen internally with a prayerful heart. What is God saying through your instinct and intuition? Today, after years of developing our intuition, if we get all ticks on our lists but a cross on the question about our gut, then we will not do whatever it is—no matter how good it looks.

God has wired us all with this extraordinary revelation infrastructure that includes intuition, instinct, hearing God, and discernment. The more we listen to Him in these ways, the easier it is to hear and the better the decisions we will make in every part of our lives. The more we push our instinct and intuition away, the harder it is to hear, and the quality of our decisions reflects this.

As we close this chapter, we encourage you to try an experiment. Look at your checklist, to-do list, or email inbox as a new way to engage with God. Turn these practical lists into a new form of prayer list. We have watched God answer practical issues and perform practical miracles over and over again. It's time for you to experience His practical solutions, ideas, and miracles in your everyday life. Partner with God on a handful of your checklists and ask Him for practical action steps. Pay attention to your intuition and instinct and remember that God has hardwired both into your very nature. God is in the business of caring for all our needs—spiritual, emotional, physical, and practical. You will begin to hear God in new ways as you choose to partner your decisions with His voice.

ACTIVATION

1. What does the Holy Spirit say to you about your current instinct and intuition gifts?
2. Can you see how these gifts have operated in your life in the past? What is one major example?

3. Name one person in your life who you can connect with about moving toward hearing God in a new way. Reach out to them.

4. What are five tangible ways that you can begin to hear God in your everyday life?

CHAPTER 6

Wisdom

The whole world is in a race for advancement. We live in a generation where everyone is trying to get the next technological breakthrough or opportunity. New markets are forming just to disrupt other markets, and they are making money at it. Success at any cost is the end goal.

We often strive for success by pursuing knowledge. People spend billions of dollars each year on seminars, coaching, education, mentorship, books, and e-courses just to advance their way of thinking so that they can hopefully be successful. We live in a culture where people sacrifice time, energy, and money on trying to hear from successful people, just hoping that as they hear from these icons of industry, they will have access to some of the wisdom and understanding that gave them those results. People are hoping that by listening to the experts, the wealthy, and the successful, their thinking will rub off on them.

What if you could have an audience with the person in your industry who was the most prominent in their field and they took a genuine interest in you, your life, and your success? What would you pay for that audience, for their wisdom and influence? People have strived to get the attention of billionaires, coaches, and celebrities for this very purpose, to glean wisdom and grow their own success. For example, every year for charity, Warren Buffet auctions off a lunch where he gives his time to someone. In 2020, the winning bid was $4.5 million and was donated to the Glide Foundation, a San Francisco-based charity.

Picture this though: As Christians, we share the same spiritual being with the most creative, most fascinating, most successful person in history: Jesus. We get to have an audience with Him anytime we want, and we can know what is in the Father's mind and heart, accessing hidden wisdom that is not common or available without Him.

The problem is, we do not always believe in our ability to have a tangible relationship with Him that will produce real revelation; but it is available! We are called to have *His* wisdom on this side of eternity, not just one day in heaven. Wisdom is one of God's most amazing attributes. The way He processes and responds to mankind is genius. He put us into the world, which is so vast that we are still discovering and exploring it. His wisdom, which He freely shares with us, teaches us how to thrive and succeed on this planet and in this life.

Pursuing knowledge and enhancing our skills are healthy practices when it comes to expanding our influence and excellence. However, knowing the mind of Christ and walking in His wisdom create profound opportunities that wouldn't exist without God. It is through God's wisdom, and a Kingdom mindset of love and servitude, that we are able to radically transform our industries and fulfill our marketplace callings.

Wisdom Is Practical and Life-Changing

On Shawn's podcast "Exploring the Prophetic," he interviewed a prayer missionary, Daniel, who became gripped with compassion every time a natural disaster struck. He felt like God was calling him to help bring relief, and so he founded the Austin Disaster Relief Network (ADRN) and began training volunteers for disaster relief and raising resources to send into areas of need.

Daniel didn't have a background in disaster relief, but God gave him the wisdom he needed to succeed at this calling. While providing relief to Hurricane Katrina victims in 2005, God gave him a vision for the network that he runs today. The network wasn't launched until four years later, but today they have donated more than $15.5 million and served more than 42,000 disaster survivors. His city and region consistently invite him to provide input for their own relief programs because they recognize the unusual wisdom on his life.

Wisdom from God creates connection, favor, and opportunity to see Jesus that would not come any other way. One of our favorite passages of scripture is 2 Chronicles 1:7-12. In this passage, God invites Solomon to "ask for whatever you want me to give you" (v. 7). Solomon asks for wisdom. The Hebrew word used here goes beyond our English understanding of wisdom. It does not just refer to knowing how to apply knowledge or to have instinct on how to build a kingdom. The Hebrew word *chokmah* means "shrewdness, skill, and prudence" as well as "to share spiritual perceptions with God," or "to share the same mind or capacity of God to lead His people." Solomon asked not just for wisdom but for the wisdom to do things the way God would—not principled wisdom, but connection to know what was in God's mind and heart.

We discussed earlier that since Jesus came and redeemed our connection to the Father, we have unlimited access to God's wisdom— because we have the very mind of Christ.

These are the things God has revealed to us by His Spirit.
The Spirit searches all things, even the deep things of

> God. For who knows a person's thoughts except their
> own spirit within them? In the same way no one knows
> the thoughts of God except the Spirit of God. What we
> have received is not the spirit of the world, but the Spirit
> who is from God, so that we may understand what God
> has freely given us. (1 Corinthians 2:10-12, NIV)

Another way to view this is that as we share God's Spirit with Him, we begin to perceive His thoughts and understand what is in the depths of His perceptions. When we ask God to communicate with us, we begin to take on His very way of thinking.

We see the example again of Solomon, where people would come from all over just to watch him rule his kingdom because he was so brilliant. This reminds us of how we watch certain people on TV, listen to TedTalks, or read self-help books. When we witness wisdom in any form, it helps us to apply it to our own lives.

We can often get caught off guard by the difference between wisdom and discernment. Discernment is understanding dynamics and the scope of things: what's good and evil, heart motives, trends, etc. Wisdom is what to do with that discernment.

Wisdom is practical and life-changing. It is the tool that shows us how we integrate this incredible spiritual life we have into our natural career, business, or opportunity.

> But the wisdom that comes from heaven is first of
> all pure; then peace-loving, considerate, submissive,
> full of mercy and good fruit, impartial and sincere.
> (James 3:17)

Solomon was so impacted by the wisdom he experienced in his life through his connection to God that he wrote Proverbs, which is still one of the books that teaches us how to reign in this life.

> My child, will you treasure my wisdom? Then, and only then, will you acquire it. And only if you accept my advice and hide it within will you succeed. So train your heart to listen when I speak and open your spirit wide to expand your discernment—then pass it on to your sons and daughters. Yes, cry out for comprehension and intercede for insight. For if you keep seeking it like a man would seek for sterling silver, searching in hidden places for cherished treasure, then you will discover the fear of the Lord and find the true knowledge of God. Wisdom is a gift from a generous God, and every word he speaks is full of revelation and becomes a fountain of understanding within you. For the Lord has a hidden storehouse of wisdom made accessible to his godly lovers. He becomes your personal bodyguard as you follow his ways, protecting and guarding you as you choose what is right. Then you will discover all that is just, proper, and fair, and be empowered to make the right decisions as you walk into your destiny. When wisdom wins your heart and revelation breaks in, true pleasure enters your soul. (Proverbs 2:1-10, TPT)

Wisdom is the thing that fills in the blanks of the questions in our lives and how to implement change. It's the substance of God that fills in the holes. Wisdom allows you to see the whole picture. Ultimately, wisdom is the knowledge on how to go forward.

Pursuing Wisdom

How do you pursue wisdom? Surround yourself with people who are wise; study and look for patterns. Most of all, pray. Like Solomon, ask God to give you wisdom and to help you grow in wisdom. In your pursuit of it, however, remember that it's a process and a journey, and that it takes time.

There are a number of ways that God supplies us with wisdom, but these are the four we see most often:

1. Connection and relationship with Him
2. His Word
3. Relationship with others
4. Your life journeys

That's not to say that young people can't be wise. We have likely all met many young people who exhibit profound wisdom. However, there is something to be said about having decades of life experience. That's why, in the pursuit of wisdom, we talk about mentors and encourage each other to find people who have gone before us who we can learn from.

When Shawn's daughter Harper was having a hard time going to sleep, he read a sleep study book to see if he could figure out how to get her to sleep regularly. Nothing was working. When he researched the author, he realized that she didn't have any kids. She was an expert in her field but she had no personal, experiential wisdom, just knowledge.

He ended up going on a message board for moms. The women on the message board would help each other by offering insight in areas that they experienced with their kids. It was incredible. Shawn found lists of things to try to help Harper sleep, and they worked. When moms on the message board mentioned the book he had been reading, not one of them gave a good review. While the book was riddled with good reviews on Amazon, he couldn't find anyone in the practical world who benefited from that author's knowledge. Instead, he found wisdom in the form of real people with real-life experience. He was able to grow in his own wisdom by learning from those who had gone before him.

The Importance of Mindset

To really understand how to build a foundation of spiritual wisdom, we need to look at the way God's people were wired to think. But we must also clear out some of our old ways of thinking as an exercise to renew our minds. We need to "set a table with our mindset." This will help disable wrong belief systems and empower our pursuit of wisdom, giving us access to the right way of thinking.

We can understand how to clear the foundation of the way we think if we look at three common mindsets: the barbarian mindset, the Greek mindset, and the Kingdom mindset.

When God called the Israelites His own in the Old Testament, He inspired them with a connection to think like He thought. He even built customs and practices that would help them succeed mentally, spiritually, and emotionally. The Hebrew (or Kingdom) mindset of the Bible is a beautiful, holistic mindset that mimics the attributes of God. It is deeply contrasted by the barbarian way of thinking, a mindset that man took on to preserve himself, to rule, and to conquer. It is also contrasted quite clearly with a Greek way of thinking.

When Christ came and reconnected us with the Father, giving us His mind, we were grafted into the Kingdom mindset and this is where we should dwell as believers. As we navigate these three mindsets, try to identify where your mindset could shift in order to further develop your understanding of spiritual wisdom in your life and marketplace role.

Survival: The Barbarian Mindset

The barbarian mindset is a "survival" mindset. Most of the Old Testament world had a barbarian way of thinking. It promotes the survival of the fittest, claiming that whoever holds power is the most important and safest. The barbarian mindset in government is measured by the ability to hold people in fear. People who are filled with fear can be easily dominated.

We see this mindset today. But we also see it in the tribal system and way of thinking in many companies and workplaces. This is the devil's favorite mindset because he came to steal, kill, and destroy, and he uses fear tactics and threats as a primary force.

In the business world, you find companies that are managed by fear, with cultures that foment the survival of the fittest, that encourage unhealthy competition, and where ideas are stolen for self-promotion. We hear of environments where employees will keep their ideas secret so that aggressive bosses or co-workers will not steal them and take the credit. These systems are rampant in companies that have not yet adopted the Kingdom mindset.

The barbarian mindset is to dominate and control, and declares that one must get one's way every time. It's a warrior who wants to overtake territories and invade other cultures without counting costs, which we see a lot in corporations or disruptive technology companies. Its motto is "We don't have to care about the environment. We don't have to care about people. We are just trying to get as much power as we can. We want to make money, not caring about how."

A barbarian mindset will destroy other people and groups for the sake of what is good for their tribe. In the marketplace, it is a dominating way of thinking and we see things like top-down management with control, fear-based systems in place, a stringent and punishing culture, and impossible metrics in order to grow within the company.

A friend of ours who works in a financial services company told us about a daily culture of fear based on the accepted practice of both co-workers and supervisors looking for areas to berate employees in order to "maintain the company culture of excellence." In other words, they were given permission to tear other people down, with the end goal of increasing productivity and reducing mistakes. In this culture, the employee turnover rate is over 70 percent.

Worshiping Man and Idols: The Greek Mindset

The Greek mindset is a thinking mindset that worships itself or mankind. In Greek thinking, faith, hope, and love are all abstract and very intangible things. This mindset focuses on abstract vision and philosophy rather than tangible reality. Greek thinking is very linear, like the subject of evolution, the big bang theory in science, or the retelling of history where customs are no longer honored with new generations because they are replaced by whatever feels right for the current people.

The Greek mindset invents new ways to express education and democracy, and each iteration can be totally independent from the last, often repeating the mistakes in hope of expressing more personal freedom. The Greek mindset tends to lean toward agnosticism and atheism because the emphasis is on the individual and not on the collective. Human reasoning is king, and a Greek mindset doesn't accept what it can't comprehend.

Pride is the root of the Greek mindset because knowledge is power. Knowledge brokering is the currency of the system and people will pay lots of money and sacrifice good character to know the right people or be connected to the right organization.

The Greek mindset makes us think we are okay while keeping us away from God's dreams for us. Paul came from this mindset, so he was often able to share with Roman citizens and people who wouldn't have listened to a more prominent Hebrew religious figure. With Paul, who understood their way of thinking, they listened and opened their hearts.

In the marketplace, we see people with a Greek mindset who are extremely independent, narcissistic, focused on personal goals above the goals of the company, opportunistic, and honoring only in the context of self-gain. This mindset within the marketplace creates a culture of comparison where people are trying to live by the book and seek perfection.

The Greek mindset also breeds a very compartmentalized way of learning. You're likely familiar with this structure: go to school to learn seven to ten distinct subjects, but there is no connection to how they relate to each other. The Greek way of thinking is also why we feel that we have a different identity at work, at home, and with friends or extracurricular activities. Oftentimes, people are separated in one area of life and self but succeed in another. Yet, the byproduct of this is a struggle with depression or unworthiness because everything feels so disjointed, even if they look like an outward success.

The Greek mindset is self-reliance, self-gratification, and humanistic love that expresses compassion that is not always connected to truth or healthy boundaries.

The Wisdom of Heaven: The Kingdom Mindset

The Kingdom mindset is one of love. It is a way of thinking that is tangibly action-based. Faith without works is dead. Jesus said, "If you love Me, keep My commandments." How do you know you have faith? By stepping out and demonstrating faith. How do you show love? By your actions.

God took the Hebrews and shaped their culture and family structure to reflect this love mindset. Their view of home, community, history, government, and life could all be seen in the spiritual viewpoint of their faith, and He gave them the Torah to define how to shape their lives around protecting this love and walking it out.

Romans 12:2 (TPT) beautifully sums up this mindset: "Stop imitating the ideals and opinions of the culture around you, but be inwardly transformed by the Holy Spirit through a total reformation of how you think. This will empower you to discern God's will as you live a beautiful life, satisfying and perfect in His eyes."

Kingdom thinking is both practical for success and prosperity and extremely healthy psychologically because it is represented by valuing your identity in family, in society, and in life, and also valuing others as yourself. The Hebrew mindset is also cyclical, as opposed to being linear. Just about all of life—the moon and solar system, the seasons, a woman's cycle, even history itself—is also cyclical, demonstrating how this mindset reflects the very creation of God. We even see this in Ecclesiastes 3:15 (NIV): "Whatever is has already been, and what will be has been before; and God will call the past to account." Understanding cycles of how God's nature looked for the generations before you will help you to succeed in your generation.

In the marketplace, when you learn to think like God, you prosper. You are not limited to your human talents, your societal position, your education, your own awareness; you have God leading you for His purpose and He can take you beyond what you hope for or imagine. The Kingdom mindset values hard work but recognizes that as you hustle, you will bear fruit that is greater than you could have produced in your own strength. As in the parable of the ten talents, there is a good God who will reward those who work with Him by multiplying what He has provided.

Another contrast of the Kingdom mindset is that it is very holistic, or non-compartmentalized. People in ancient Judaism were apprenticed in the ways of culture, and each subject they learned was taught thoroughly and connected to other subjects. In that way, they would learn how each topic impacted their home life, their place in society, and their job. The religion itself didn't lend to compartmentalization or dissociation. To truly love God with all their heart, mind, and strength, they had to be connected in all those areas to themselves and the world around them; that was the proof of the love.

Leaning into the Kingdom Mindset

One of the things that God promises us when we follow Him is that we won't have to lean on our own understanding and we can be whole people. When people are compartmentalized, they do not believe they will hear from God in areas where they aren't feeling empowered. It is hard to feel strong in wisdom when you have multiple areas of life breaking down. Even if you have something that is going well, the pain and weak areas will still overshadow that success. One example is when a person is incredibly famous and successful but gets divorced and struggles to be a good parent. They do not go to bed at night enjoying the glory of their life; they usually end up with coping mechanisms and in deep emotional depression.

When we don't have a Kingdom mindset, we have a hard time accessing God and others relationally. Instead, we end up trying to hear His voice to get ahead in life and not to grow in our Christlikeness. Our agendas are birthed out of our mindset and many good Christians in the marketplace can be barbarian or Greek thinkers, especially in the way they work.

With the Kingdom mindset, we do our jobs so that the fruit is the same fruit we are meant to demonstrate in our daily lives: "But the fruit of the Spirit is love, joy, peace, forbearance, kindness, goodness, faithfulness, gentleness and self-control. Against such things there is no law" (Galatians 5:22-23).

When consulting, Bob often runs into those who are exhibiting a mindset of comparison, promotion, and self-interest instead of the fruit of the Spirit. This is often evident in younger businesspeople who are discouraged because they feel like they should be a millionaire before they are thirty. When he asks them, "Where did you hear that?" invariably the answer is "social media." They are simply replicating the mindset that they are seeing on their newsfeeds.

The truth is, once someone is out of high school or college, he or she has an approximate working career of forty to fifty years. When a twenty-five-year-old is feeling shame because "everyone else is making it," Bob reminds them that there is a long road ahead of them. Most young people have not even worked 10 percent of their working career and they are already being pulled into a comparison and discouraged mindset. Temperance and patience are virtues that we must have for this long road and are a byproduct of the Kingdom mindset.

> Do you not know that in a race all the runners run, but only one gets the prize? Run in such a way as to get the prize. Everyone who competes in the games goes into strict training. They do it to get a crown that will not last, but we do it to get a crown that will last forever. (1 Corinthians 9:24-25, NIV)

Wisdom Breeds Hope and Transformation

As a Christian in the marketplace, your calling is like that of Joseph, Daniel, Esther, and Paul—to shine from the highest lamp stand you can stand on so that people can see what Jesus looks like through your life. Your calling is to bring transformation to the culture around you.

Success is a secondary goal and often a byproduct of transformation. When we pursue wisdom and a Kingdom mindset, the overall aim is transformation. The Greek mindset, however, puts success and personal gain above seeing lives and culture actually transformed.

When we start to connect deeply to the wisdom of the Father of heaven, we become aware of His original agenda on the earth. Things start to click inside of us and the "why" for whatever we are working on becomes clearer—or at least the answer to "Why am I alive?" starts to get fleshed out.

Our first job, role, or business is most likely going to be extremely hard. We are going to do the jobs that other people do not want to do. We are going to be underpaid. If we are patient, committed, and seek God's wisdom, we will bear a harvest; the Bible promises that. The problem is, the harvest is not always financial. Sometimes it is significance, position in community, activism, stewarding land and resources, being a trustworthy person.

God has planted Himself in seasons of our lives, and things take time to develop in us. God is not in a hurry or Jesus would have already returned. If we are going to access God's wisdom for our business, His voice is not here for our immediate gratification. He is here to work with us, in us, and then through us. He is developing us to become like Him. This is His ultimate wisdom that we get to rest in over and over again.

The hyper-wealth movement in America, and also perpetuated by the church, waters down so many of our goals. We hurry to gain our American dream, wealth, and success, oftentimes bypassing opportunities on the way that God has called us to be present in.

This is where a life filled with God's wisdom will set us apart. Even in the trials, when we must wait for God to use circumstances for our good (see Romans 8:28), we can walk with hope, character, and connection.

People who do not have this hope live in survival mode, holding their breath and on pause. You, however, have access to the wisdom and hope of God, even when things are not working for you or even if they are working against you. This is what wisdom does: it grounds us in the Father's desires and plan for our lives, instead of our own plans and thoughts. There is a moment of surrender in wisdom, when we realize we are not in control and we don't have to be in control to be happy.

God ultimately wants to share His perspective with you, to coach you through His Spirit, to help your life be a conduit of transformation—where the things around you are restored to His original design and desire. You are a powerful person of wisdom when you spend time getting to know Him. Just as wisdom and Kingdom thinking brought a distinction to Solomon's life and to Jesus' life, so too your life will be set apart because of your ability to hear God and manage His perspective through your career.

Taking the time to listen to God for your career, business, decisions, and dreams is valuable. Our society says that we must conquer our fears, take control of our situation, and make life happen for ourselves. The Kingdom of heaven says, "Trust in the Lord with all your heart, and do not lean on your own understanding, in all your ways acknowledge Him, and He will make your paths straight" (Proverbs 3:5-6, NASB).

When we fully understand the privilege of our connection with the

Father—the ability to invite Him into hard decisions, listen to His still small voice, listen to what He says through our friends, mentors and advisers—we will hear the wisdom of heaven in a new and practical way.

ACTIVATION

1. Can you think of a time when God gave you supernatural wisdom in a circumstance? Or a time when you had wisdom that you knew was not inherent to your skill, degree, or life experience and must have come from God?
2. What fruits of the Spirit do you currently see in your life?
3. What is one practical thing you can do today to move away from survival thinking?
4. When you connect to God, what is your purpose for being alive? What is your mission in life?

CHAPTER 7

Agenda

As Christians, we are called to be people of purpose. We have been given the tools, resources, and even a plan of action (see Matthew 28). Without purpose, it is easy to get divided in our focus or even to become unmotivated. Proverbs 29:18 puts it this way: "When there is no clear prophetic vision, people quickly wander astray. But when you follow the revelation of the word, heaven's bliss fills your soul."

Being people of purpose goes beyond having a plan for our lives and walking it out. It is one thing to *have* a purpose but another thing to be purposeful. When we try to fulfill one without the other, our actions become distorted by hidden agendas.

Our friend Julie, who is in the beauty industry in film, went on set the other day for work. One of the other ladies in her field came in as well. Julie approaches her occupation as service to Jesus, but she knows she cannot have an extroverted evangelical agenda or she won't be hired back. So, she chooses to influence those around her through excellence in her work.

The other girl who came in that day approached her work with a sense of urgency and huge personality, but it was not about the work she came to perform; she had an ulterior motive. She had started her own product line and was pushing it on everyone she was serving. It created tension because her agenda was not what she was being paid to do. As a matter of fact, it violated the atmosphere, and everyone was frustrated.

Julie said the girl was completely unaware of how toxic the atmosphere had become. She probably had a great dream and passion, but she was expressing it in a way that violated others and was hindering her goal rather than supporting it. On set, she looked at Julie and said, "You can get in on the ground floor and be in on my own product line!"— except that the product was not as good as what they were requested to use on set, and it showed.

This woman was using her place of influence with a secondary agenda and it was obvious to those around her. She was not brought back the next day. They told her agency they did not want her. This is a picture of what happens when we have a secondary agenda that violates our primary agenda or purpose. Her primary purpose on set was to serve the cast of the film with great care and excellent beauty products. Yet, she wasn't purposeful in that role, allowing her secondary agenda to overpower her purpose.

Reveal Your Agenda

We would like to propose that everyone has an agenda. While the word "agenda" has many negative connotations, it really just refers to having an underlying ideology or plan. Everyone who has a vision has an agenda, but many Christians think it is humility to pretend that we do not have one, because aren't we servants to all? The problem is, if we don't define our purpose and clearly communicate it when needed, then we will operate—even unwittingly—out of hidden agendas, which are destructive to the environment and relationships around us.

As we get a vision and set goals for our lives, this agenda helps us to filter out God opportunities from those things that may appear good but will take us off course. Being purposeful in that calling is what helps us avoid pursuing hidden agendas.

We've all been burned by people who come to us with ulterior motives or hidden agendas, whether religious or otherwise. It is painful when people invite us to spend time with them only to find out later that they had a hidden agenda.

Having a pure heart is to live without a hidden agenda. One of the beautiful things about God is that He discloses the mysteries of the Kingdom to the poor in spirit, the meek, and those who have nothing. There's nothing hidden in God.

We often get an opportunity or an idea and, in our eagerness, want to draft people into it. But if we aren't careful, we can bring something to the table while missing regular social cues, or we aren't upfront and honest about what we need because we fear confrontation. There are many things that can hinder our goal of being pure and without ulterior motives. By not being purposeful with our agenda or vision, however, we make others feel ambushed. Those ambushes can cost us relationship, time, and energy.

For those of us who come from a background in sales, some of the most underhanded tactics of agenda are taught. Multi-level marketing, for example, often teaches you to be indirect in your agenda, but this approach can violate the trust you've built with those you are reaching out to.

Unfortunately, this becomes learned behavior that we then express in many of our interactions at work, church, in business meetings, and in our relationships. We see this when someone invites us to a seemingly casual conversation only to find out they want to confront us about something. That is a hidden agenda in action, and it feels violating.

The same is true when we use these tactics to approach someone about faith. They feel hoodwinked and their walls immediately go up, defeating the purpose of our agenda in the first place.

We both often get approached to discuss business opportunities, and it can go one of two ways: People explain upfront why they would like to meet, which gives us the opportunity to decline, or they invite us out without revealing their motives.

This happened just a few weeks ago. An old friend of Shawn's, whom he hadn't seen in a long time, called and said he wanted to catch up. Shawn was excited to meet with him. When the time came, however, the friend just wanted to give Shawn a sales pitch. It's in those moments that you feel violated because it feels as though the other person only sees your involvement as financially smart or a way to increase followers.

The exact opposite thing happened when another friend asked Shawn to lunch. The request was out of the blue, so Shawn called him back and asked, "What's your agenda?"

"What?" he said.

"What do you want to talk about?"

Shawn's friend laughed and said, "I just wanted to have lunch."

"Okay," Shawn said, "so you're not going to talk to me about multi-level marketing, or this or that?"

He laughed again and said, "What's the matter with you? You have obviously been abused by some people."

In our marketplace purpose, it is important to walk in purity and humility, and that looks like openly sharing whether or not we have an agenda—if it is even appropriate to use that opportunity to pursue your agenda. In some cases, it is not.

The same is true of our Kingdom purposes. Instead of ambushing those around us with our agenda of faith, we have learned to ask friends or co-workers if we can share something about our faith that may be relevant to their situation. When you set expectations, you have healthy boundaries in relationships. When you don't set boundaries, and you come to a situation needing something from the other person, it becomes obvious right away.

We can also apply this principle in reverse. When we understand our purpose and others come to us with an agenda—hidden or otherwise—we can better navigate our involvement in that opportunity. When people approach us with clear expectations and nothing hidden, it is so much easier to say, "Yes! I want to be involved," or "No, this isn't my assignment, but thanks for sharing."

Navigating Agendas in the Workplace

Making your agenda or purpose clear is important. When we hear from God in the workplace, the job God enables us to do, as well as the way we do it, should be a message of encouragement to those around us. Sharing our faith in the marketplace can have a similar effect. When we do have those moments of sharing our spiritual journey, it should be inviting people into a conversation, not afflicting them with our opinions or lifestyle.

Bolz Ministries offers personal prayer services for some of our business partner friends. This has happened around twenty-five times over the years where they'll put together a spiritual night for people who are interested in spirituality and say, "We want to have a night where we have invited Christian ministers to pray for you. They hear from God and it's always exciting to see what God will say."

Some have added, "This is going to be weird for a lot of you and we don't want you to judge us for this." And one of them even said, "Hey, this might be like, maybe you've gone to tarot readings or a medium or a psychic. Well, as Christians, God speaks, and some people hear Him in powerful ways and it's amazing. And you do not have to come, but if you do, you might be put on the spot, but it is just going to be a fun night. We're going to host a dinner."

The business leaders will invite their teams, people who they are building a relationship with, and then bring us in as trusted friends. There is a lot less at stake because these evenings take place outside of the workplace. There are no surprises for the guests because the business leader or manager creates clear expectations of a spiritual and entertaining night that is not just about connecting or networking. And it has worked well every time we have done this.

The thing we love about this strategy is that guests are invited with a clear agenda and no pressure to come.

The book *Business of Honor* discusses the importance of this approach to building relationship with those in our lives, especially in the workplace: "Genuine influence that wins the hearts of people is not achieved by charismatic speeches, but by breaking off a piece of our lives and offering it to others. For this reason, we must be careful to follow David's advice to Solomon: 'Above all else, guard your heart, for everything you do flows from it.'"

The book goes on to describe a self-evaluation to help us be honoring, authentic leaders and influencers in the workplace, and in our personal lives. When we choose to be honest and trustworthy in our approach to all our relationships, we become better leaders, co-workers, and friends and are able to identify when we are functioning from an agenda instead of relationship and heart connection.

> Leaders must realize that there is no neutral ground; they are either actively choosing honor or falling into dishonor, actively pursuing the goal of connection or

defaulting toward the goal of disconnection. This means they should have a habit of doing regular self-checks and relationship checks—what I call "keeping current" with myself and people so that any fear or disconnection is swiftly identified and dealt with. Here are a few questions that should be part of an honoring leader's habitual self and relationship checks:

"Do I see myself ..." (self-check) and "Do you see me ..." (relationship check):

- Pursuing the goal of connection, especially with those closest to me, or have I allowed fear to convince me to start creating distance with anyone?
- Communicating the truth in love to people, or am I either hiding or hurting people with the truth?
- Consistently seeking feedback from trusted sources, or avoiding feedback?
- Being comfortable, or resisting confrontation?
- Taking risks to grow and learn, or allowing the fear of failure or being seen as incompetent to hold me back?
- Needing to clean up any messes?
- Focusing too much on the short-term?

(*Business of Honor*, p. 153)

Your God-Given Purpose

One of the most common agendas that Christians have inner conflict about is what we already briefly discussed: the role of evangelism at work. Each of us has the God-given purpose to love our neighbor, but all too often we see people express their agenda about their Christian faith in a way that violates their primary directives to work efficiently. This behavior becomes a liability to them at their workplace. Or they put requirements on people around them to operate out of defined biblical character in ways that just do not make sense to the other person.

So, what is our purpose in the marketplace and how do we avoid creating agendas that violate that purpose?

Apart from remaining pure of heart and honest, one way to avoid hidden agendas, or really any agenda that violates the purposes of God, is to remind ourselves of this one thing: we don't have to turn the workplace into church. That would be a mistake. Instead, we must learn to demonstrate the nature of God to those around us by purposing to fulfill the task He has given us.

There was a business owner that Shawn knew who wanted all his employees to refrain from using the Lord's name in vain not only at work but also at home. That created a sense of control and confusion for his employees who felt micromanaged about something they did not even understand. Most of his work friends were no longer returning his calls and he didn't understand how his secondary agenda had spoiled his primary God-given purpose of running a successful business.

What he didn't understand at the time is that God isn't holding sinners accountable for saying His name in vain; they don't even know what that means. To focus on that as a major issue simply created a problem where there previously hadn't been one. In fact, it was an agenda founded on fear—fear that the employees weren't living free of sin or compromise.

Hidden and fear-based agendas have a way of revealing themselves, however. Another gentleman who worked at an energy company as a manager would start the company meetings with a fifteen-minute Bible study. Eventually, the owners, who didn't have the same biblical values, began to feel that forty-five minutes a month of their employees' work time was wasted. They kindly confronted the manager and asked him to only have his Bible studies at lunch, not during work meetings. He could not see their argument's merit and ended up underperforming because of conflicting agendas. It was self-inflicted pain.

What does it look like, however, when we approach our work with a love-based agenda and the purposes of God? A friend of ours has a regular series of Bible studies once a week at lunch time at a major Hollywood studio. She also hosts a meal for the homeless each week and invites friends from work—especially those who may not go to a Bible study—to hang out with her Christian friends at one of their street dinners. That creates a safe space and a place of value for her co-workers to be exposed to Christ outside of work in a neutral environment that gives everyone self-esteem as they work on an issue of social justice together.

Another friend of ours pursues his love-based agenda while running a Fortune 500 company. He shows his value for his staff by paying for an extravagant retreat every year to advance his leaders' vision, mission, and goals. At some point, he shares what he is learning, which is often tied to his faith, and even the most anti-Christian people who come often leave buzzing with excitement and renewed perspective on the company and some have accepted Jesus because of this sacrificial retreat.

Our God-given agenda, in alignment with good work ethic and values, does not violate the culture around us. We mentioned Joseph as an example of Kingdom influence. Joseph was given a powerful agenda for his people when he was brought into Pharaoh's house. God gave him influence so that Joseph could use his leverage to keep his people safe.

However, in order to receive the protection of Egypt through Joseph, the Israelites had to serve Egypt. As you can imagine, that decision was probably incredibly controversial. Joseph was able to provide them with protection from the famine, but at a cost. The Israelites, his brothers and family, could have judged him. The same people he was trying to save could have said, "You've sold us into slavery. You're selling us out because you want to be our leader!"

Somehow, though, they recognized Joseph's influence and God's hand of grace, and they chose to humbly accept Joseph's help. Part of that acceptance was due to Joseph walking out his God-given purpose and agenda in a way that didn't violate those he was serving.

Likewise, Joseph served Pharaoh with such integrity that Pharaoh never questioned Joseph's motives. When Joseph came forward with his agenda for his people and his own family, Pharaoh immediately let him have it. Joseph always knew that he would be in a place of influence for his people. He knew that God loved His people and he expected Him to come through. Joseph wasn't surprised when he received his position, nor that God used that position to bless others. We need to expect the same. God is giving us a purpose—and an agenda—to fulfill in our areas of influence. When we set aside fear and walk out our agenda in confidence and love, God's purposes are always revealed.

What Is Your Marketplace Agenda?

Everyone needs to be shown love and everyone desires purpose. When we approach our work with this in mind, it is easy to see opportunities to express Christ's agenda without inserting our own. We see this so clearly in our modern-day sports franchises. Many teams are inviting chaplains to be available to their players. Some of these chaplains have been a singular lifeline to the players and invaluable in times of crisis.

Our primary mandate as a Christian is to love, and then we have the great commission: to make disciples of all men. Love must come first in leading us, and that means we must have self-awareness and emotional intelligence for how and when to evangelize and "make disciples." Wisdom tells us that we can't bring faith up in every conversation and that there is a time and place for it. It in no way means we separate our faith journey from work, just that our goals are in the right order.

Evangelism isn't always an overt expression of Christian theology. In many cases, it is demonstrated as we purpose to hear God and do the work He has called us to. We often associate being cared for and pastored with attending church. Yet, all people need to be cared for and loved in every area of life, whether they are believers or not. What better place to show people the tangible love of God than in their everyday lives at work? It is this practical experience that allows people to encounter Christ through us—not just on Sunday through prayer ministry—but every day through lived-out love and compassion.

ACTIVATION

1. Can you identify your marketplace agenda?
2. Can you identify any hidden agendas you might have?
3. How can you reformat your agendas with God's Kingdom attributes?
4. In what ways can you support the people around you in what God has called you to do?

CHAPTER 8

Transform

On a recent trip to Singapore, Shawn observed one of the most pristine visions—from a design and development standpoint—of a city and country in our generation. Everything from the physical visual identity of the nation in its architecture and layout to the transportation systems, agriculture, and artistry represented cultural transformation.

The founding father and first prime minister of the modern, independent iteration of Singapore was named Lee Kuan Yew. People called him an architect of culture and he took the ideas he formed and used them to transform Singapore from a developing nation into a small world power. There are many aspects of Singapore's history and current government structure that are controversial, too much to cover here. What is intriguing, however, is how one nation could so rapidly develop in one generation around very humanistic principles of governance and economy. If that is possible, then what could happen when Kingdom-minded believers, empowered by God, choose to transform the culture around them?

What Does Transformation Look Like?

We discussed cultural transformation under Solomon, who organized Israel to be a world power in one generation, a symbol of the Messiah and His reign. That is why so many people thought that Jesus was going to be a king in the natural and do what Solomon did. But He had a better plan. He architected internal culture so that His Kingdom wouldn't come and go with trends of governments and education but would be deeply rooted spiritually inside all of us, always budding and growing from one believer to another. He created a viral Kingdom whose most potent property is the message of love.

His original plan is still the same: to bring restoration not just over us individually but also over nations, regions, industries, and the environment. We are created with the instinct and revelation to connect to these original thoughts and desires of God, transforming culture, connecting people to Him, and aligning our industries to the original pattern God meant for them to display.

There have been cities that have experienced a move of God realigning leadership and priorities with Kingdom themes. Back in the 1990s the Sentinel Group put out a series of videos asking this question: What happens when a city dedicates itself to God? They had fascinating research and video showing how several third-world nations were experiencing a healing of their physical land and agricultural, social issues, justice systems, addiction rates, etc. Our entire generation of leadership in the church rushed to watch the videos because all of us knew that Jesus wasn't just promised a few people as His reward and inheritance; He was promised generations, cities, and nations.

Transformation comes in many different forms. We've seen the personal transformation of individuals or co-workers, cultural change in a single business, and the transformation of entire regions. When Bill

Gates chose to move Microsoft to Washington, for example, instead of Silicon Valley, he also brought with him transformation for the Redmond/Seattle area. He loved Washington and wanted it to prosper, and it did. Microsoft became one of the largest employers in the area, providing jobs and boosting the economy by attracting other businesses to the state.

When we dream of God transformation, we should dream big. When we consider all the things that God has put inside of us, it should come as no surprise that we can change cities, regions, and the people we come into contact with every single day. And when we invite that same mindset into the marketplace, transformation should be in everything we do and touch. We carry the ability to transform things just by being us, doing what we are called to do, and walking with Jesus.

Many of you are likely familiar with the story of Magnolia Market. When Chip and Joanna Gaines started Magnolia Market in 2003, they couldn't imagine they would one day transform their entire town of Waco, Texas. In fact, they closed the shop in 2006 in order to pursue their construction business and Joanna laid down her dream of owning a boutique. When their construction work got picked up by HGTV, however, everything changed. Eight years after shutting it down, not only did Joanna restart her store, but they transformed two city blocks of abandoned property into shops, restaurants, and entertainment space, turning Waco into a tourist destination. They transformed their city by following God's grace and call on their lives, and they are also influencing lives all over the world through their own TV network, cookbooks, children's books, and more. Their heart for their local town, as well as their passion for people and design, have made them a household name. God loves to use people who will lean into Him to transform the world.

Transformation begins with us choosing to connect with God's heart for our lives and purpose. The end result is often something far more than we can imagine. When Walt Disney began making films, for example, he believed that every child should have a place where they could experience joy and become dreamers, which was the opposite of the belief in that era that children should be seen and not heard.

In a conversation with Walt's producer, Ken Wales, Shawn learned that faith played a huge role in all of Walt Disney's decisions and the things he built. One thing Disney told Ken was that in creating a place for children to experience joy, he didn't want to create Bible Land. At one time, he had thought about a Bible-themed park, with rides created around characters like Esther and Daniel and King David. But he realized that this would exclude children of other faiths. He knew that God's heart was for every child and so he wanted to create a place where every child could experience the joy of being a child. His solution was to create Disneyland.

The legacy of Walt Disney still impacts our lives to this day. He transformed the culture to see childlike joy as a blessing and invited generations of children of all backgrounds to experience the delight of being kids. We imagine that when he first got the inspiration for Mickey Mouse, Walt Disney had no idea how pursuing his passion would bring about such tremendous transformation.

This type of transformation isn't just happening through entertainment and retail or design, but in all sectors and even in government. When we choose to live out our Kingdom values and partner with God, transformation touches everything we do. Even those who are completely unfamiliar with God and His ways can recognize the power of transformation on our lives.

The Chinese government recently went to a Christian charismatic college called Wagner Leadership Institute and asked them to come to their nation to start an official theological seminary in China. The leaders of China recognize that they have so much corruption and a lack of loyalty and faithfulness, and they need a solution. The answer they chose: Western Christianity. It was the only solution they could find that would help govern business and military leaders with the virtues of honor, humility, and honesty. Even China recognizes the impact that Christianity can have on normal society.

These are all examples of incredible cultural transformation, but it doesn't end there. What does transformation look like for us today, in our jobs, careers, and businesses? The idea of transforming a city or nation can seem hugely overwhelming, but transformation often starts small. It starts with us.

We are not into hyper-dominion theology where the whole earth will be perfected, and then Jesus will come, and we will rule every place of influence. As a matter of fact, our role, even in transformation, is to come as servants, just as Daniel, Joseph, Esther, and Jesus demonstrated. We are not all to be king of the mountain, but to influence through our love and humility. This does not mean we won't find ourselves in places of leadership and incredible influence. It does mean, however, that transformation looks like servitude and love, no matter what our role, demonstrating the rule and reign of only one: Jesus.

John 3:17 (MSG) says it best: "God did not go to all the trouble of sending his Son merely to point an accusing finger, telling the world how bad it was. He came to help, to put the world right again." When you believe that God so loved the world that He gave His Son, and then see that He wants to put the world right again, that should seriously change your vantage point on your career and the transformation you can bring.

People Will Know God by How You Do Business

When people view a life in Christ that is partnered to Him, it causes wonder. We are supposed to give people a glimpse of what eternity is like through our lives, not just through our vocalized love, not just through our message. Our life preaches. The way we live our life and what we do brings redemptive and transformative components to our careers, industries, and relationships, and preaches who Jesus is.

When Shawn was in South Korea years ago, he met a businessman who worked in the automobile industry. The man had a vision of an invention that he didn't understand. He drew it out and showed his engineers in his company and they knew what it might be. They created a prototype of it, and it was an emissions device that would actually significantly reduce emissions in vehicles in a way that had never been done.

That alone was an incredible miracle. But the businessman didn't stop there. Because the new invention brought in so many contracts and an increase of funding, he made sure this affected his employees' well-being and blessed everyone in his company in practical, financial ways. Not just then, but he created a pattern of giving to his employees whenever he had a breakthrough.

Hardly any were Christians when they first started their jobs, but after years of his amazing father heart, the whole company got saved. When Shawn met the businessman, his company was holding prayer meetings every morning to start the day—powerful prayer meetings that felt like Pentecostal church meetings in the middle of a factory. The businessman has also been able to share with other business and government leaders in India and China over and over about his faith because everyone wanted to know how he had come upon the technology, and he could only point to God.

What if, in your career, people would know there's a God because they've met you? What if simply knowing you brings about transformation? Have you ever met somebody who is so brilliant in what they do that you just can't get enough of them? What are some of the qualities that you admire most about that person?

It isn't just being kind or financially generous that draws people to see God in you. Demonstrating the fruit of the Spirit in your everyday interactions and business transactions has a powerfully transformational effect on others. Sometimes the simple act of displaying God's character in the workplace is enough to bring cultural transformation wherever you go.

We see this played out in the example of Chick-fil-A. The company demonstrates integrity and honor in how they train their employees, source their chicken, and treat their customers. They challenge the entire fast-food industry to be more excellent by displaying excellence on every level, from the flow of cars through their drive-thru to the processes in place to make sure customers get exactly what they ordered. On top of that, they are closed on Sundays because they wanted to make a value statement to their employees. It's not for the world but for their employees to have a day of rest.

Chick-fil-A rose to prominence simply by living out Kingdom principles through practical business practices. It's a picture of transformation, causing an entire industry to question their own best practices because of the demonstration of the Father and His character.

Some of these transformational characteristics include:

1. Honesty
2. Responsibility
3. Ownership
4. Excellence
5. Honor
6. Trust
7. Love
8. Authenticity
9. Wisdom

Let's look at another example of demonstrating the Kingdom by how we do business. Joseph, Jesus' stepdad, was a carpenter and a good man. Imagine what it was like when Joseph did his job. Was it done right and in such a timely manner that it was the most beautiful craftsmanship that people had experienced? When Jesus was on the earth, there were probably people in His community who proudly said, "Oh, His dad made my house." And their Yelp review would have been extremely excited, saying, "He was amazing. So that makes so much sense that Jesus is who He is."

Jesus was only in the ministry for approximately three and a half years, starting at age thirty. Until he was thirty, He would have worked as a carpenter with His father. Could you imagine Him walking onto your job site? What would that be like? If He said it would be done in a day, it would be. If He said He would fix something, He would. He made no mistakes, and He was economically just. People probably adored His business side because through His integrity, He was reflecting the Father.

Let's imagine His business for a moment. What happened when His crew made a mistake? He wouldn't try to cover it up or up-charge; He knew how to take responsibility. Or He wouldn't try to overcharge a job in a wealthier part of town that He would do at a lesser rate in a poorer part. He would have paid His employees fairly and cared about their lives outside of work.

We all have potential to be otherworldly in our career. When you meet a Christian who has wisdom and connection to themselves and the heart of God, you feel like God is embodied in their career, business, and gifting.

Embodying God and bringing transformation in this way is our destiny. The world is asking Christians: What makes you so special? Does loving God actually make a difference in your real life and purpose, or is it all a ritual and an empty religion? It's time to show the world the transformational power of Christ.

Feedback Is a Key to Transformation

When we discussed instinct and intuition, we also touched on the importance of involving your team or trusted advisers in your decisions. Feedback is a powerful tool for cultural transformation. Why? Because it requires vulnerability and helps build connection with those around us.

If we're using our instinct and intuition, that means that we're stepping out in risk to bring about change or make a profound decision. By involving others, we're setting aside our agendas and allowing input and wisdom from Jesus, business partners, mentors, colleagues, and our spouse.

And that is part of transformation: creating a culture that is honest, vulnerable, and powerful.

> Healthy feedback is assertively giving an account of the way we are experiencing another person, or receiving such an account from another person about the way they are experiencing us, in order to meet the needs of our relationship and our shared mission. An honoring approach to exchanging feedback sends the message, "I care about you, and I care about our relationship. I want and need to know how you are experiencing me, and I am willing to adjust my behavior to create the experience you need to be having with me. I also promise to give you great information about how I am experiencing you, because I trust that you share the same value for me and our relationship, and I don't expect you to read my mind or anticipate my needs unless I communicate them." (*Business of Honor*, p. 113)

In the past, we didn't use the term "feedback" in the marketplace. Instead, we called it "constructive criticism" and it was often maligned. The term "constructive criticism" feels like you're going to hear negative things about yourself or the way you do your job. By using the word "feedback," we open ourselves up to the idea that receiving input from others is a positive thing and something that leads to positive transformation.

In our modern era, we get a false sense of feedback from our social networks and technology. Instead of seeking face-to-face, vulnerable input, we use likes and shares as our feedback as to whether or not something works. However, this doesn't support lasting change or transformation. When Bob started his business, face-to-face contact was the primary way to interact, and if that wasn't possible, then the next option was a phone call. Today, with text messages and DMs, we no longer have to even talk to people. But what would it say to those around you if you put relationship above technology and authentic feedback above social media engagement in both your life and your career?

Imagine for a moment your favorite restaurant. What makes it your favorite? Likely the food plays a role, but there are a lot of restaurants serving great food. In many cases, you are drawn to a favorite restaurant because of its environment. When you walk down a street where there are multiple restaurants but only a few are thriving, those that are thriving have created an environment that is inviting, one that people want to spend their time enjoying.

Our lives should be so transformed that we create an environment that people want to be part of. That transformation will then leak out into our jobs, our passions, and our relationships. If this is not our current reality, then how do we get to the point where people want to be in our environment in both work and life? Start with feedback. If we're not creating culture or bringing transformation, it might be because our own transformation hasn't happened yet.

As we seek God's original plan and desire, we have to crave feedback. It allows us to grow, strengthen, and bring even greater transformation in the future. It also allows us to demonstrate God's gentle way of correcting through honesty and kindness. In many ways, seeking feedback in business and life sets us apart in our careers and influence, and that in itself brings transformation.

ACTIVATION

1. How are you connecting with God's heart and purpose today?
2. Can you invite Jesus in what you are called to do and identify what God is transforming?
3. Who are people in your life that you allow to give you honest feedback?
4. How can you implement small practical changes to see transformation in one area of your life?

CHAPTER 9

Perspective

Great men and women of God have an eternal perspective. Perspective is one of the most powerful prophetic tools we have. It is the ability to ground ourselves in the bigger picture of eternity even when we might be facing failure in the present. As a matter of fact, perspective can turn a seemingly obvious failure into a glowing success.

Perspective helps us to view things in their relative importance and to see the truth of the circumstance and not just the potential outcome. Why is this important? Perspective is the main factor in determining how an event resonates with you, how you feel about a situation, and how you will remember what happened. It is your ability to process the world around you and what is happening in your inside world with God. When you have a healthy perspective, you can face incredible odds and still come out not just with a positive spin or outlook but also in deeply grounded truth about God, the world, and your place in it.

There was a young woman with whom Bob was consulting who had a difficult boss. After months of hemming and hawing about quitting her job, Bob invited her to do an experiment. He told her that she should start praying for her boss.

When she asked what he meant, he said, "I think you should just start praying for her because most people aren't mean; most people aren't evil; most people aren't trying to hurt you."

She seemed a little taken aback. "But this woman is," she said.

"I understand," Bob continued. "So why don't you do a two-week experiment and pray for her?"

A week into the experiment, things started to shift. The young woman told Bob, "Wow! My boss hasn't changed at all, but my heart has. I feel my perspective has changed. My heart is different toward this woman."

She decided to take the experiment further than two weeks because it had so profoundly helped her shift her perspective. Sometime after the two weeks were up, her boss came in one day looking terrible. The young woman, who now had over two weeks of compassion built up, looked at her boss and said, "Are you okay? I've been praying for you for two and a half weeks. Is something happening that I can pray for you about?"

The boss looked at her and said, "You've been praying for me?" And when the woman replied yes, the boss invited her to lunch.

This young woman discovered that her boss had experienced some trauma in her family that she'd been trying to manage. It was getting worse and worse right around the time period when the young woman started praying for her. The fact that this employee had compassion changed the boss's perspective and her view of her employee. Over time, this young girl became her boss's confidant. All it took for the situation to change was an eternal, love-based perspective.

The Importance of Interdependence on Perspective

Higher perspective comes out of deeper relationship. The more trusted advisers and friends we have, with humility in our hearts toward them, the clearer our path becomes. God-given relationships, which the Bible often refers to as covenant relationships, are essential in a marketplace life. They have purpose and commitment in the Kingdom and create a multiplication effect.

Jesus walked with the twelve disciples and created friendships within their circle because He knew they would need each other. He constantly pointed out the importance of unity and friendship, saying, "For where two or three gather in my name, there am I with them" (Matthew 18:20). He made us interdependent on each other just as He modeled being interdependent on His Father and the Holy Spirit.

Independence and self-reliance breed disconnection and fear. When Shawn's ministry went through one of its hardest times financially—it grew so fast that it created cash flow problems—Bob stepped in to help. As a marketplace person, it is easy to look at metrics that, with your own natural eyes, can only mean one thing. In the natural, things did not look good for the ministry. But with eyes of others, you can see options that weren't previously on the table.

When Bob stepped in, he told Shawn, "I'm not sure why you are going to be okay, but you are going to be okay." Bob was forecasting with them, so he knew the metrics and the financials of what was coming and where the ministry stood. While he was looking at the data, he also carried a perspective like Joseph, where he could feel the breakthrough that was ahead if the ministry continued in faith. He brought the perspective of a father, a brother, and a business leader and it was stabilizing. If the ministry had been alone, they would have slowed down some areas and probably crashed financially.

Together, we learn how to walk more intimately in godly perspective, choosing not to be rooted just in the analytics but also in a place of faith and connection. The more trusted advisers and friends we open our hearts to, the clearer our path becomes.

This is also a principle central to Jewish culture. When you were born or brought into relationship in biblical days, you became part of a much wider family. If you needed a shoe fixed, they would send you to Cousin Abe. If you needed a shepherd, they would send you to their great-uncle Boaz. There existed a resourcing of family, which provided the perspective that you were not alone. This is a huge component of why our Christian perspective is unique: we now belong to a family of God that is worldwide and supportive of one another.

Interdependence also helps maintain a healthy perspective in our lives, families, and careers. Years ago, Bob went through a period of confusion and burnout and lost his global perspective. He needed to step back to gain his 30,000-foot perspective. What this entailed was taking extended time off from the operations of the company and actually trusting those he had in place to manage the day-to-day operations. He took a two-week trip to a lodge in Arizona with no cell coverage, where he took time to rest, exercise, and recharge. He was able to hear the still small voice of God again as he rested. A few things happened on this retreat/sabbatical:

1. His office and field staff flourished and took care of the operations of the company.
2. He recognized that God was fully in control of his life, family, and business.
3. His priorities were reset by spending this time away with God.

In today's society of being digitally connected at all times, we are more susceptible to fatigue, burnout, moral failure, and crashes. When stepping away for rest isn't feasible, there are other ways to avoid burnout and a loss of perspective. In his book *The Ten Signs of a Leadership*

Crash, author Stephen Mansfield lists signs that we should look for in ourselves and our friends in order to help each other maintain a healthy perspective:

1. Being out of season
2. Choosing isolation
3. Defining episodes of bitterness
4. Evading confrontation
5. Losing trusted friendships
6. Forgetting fun
7. Perpetuating an artificial image
8. Serving the schedule
9. Building a third world
10. Losing the poetry

If we are able to have good, honest perspective in our lives and see perspective in our friends and family, we will be able to avoid these indicators before we or someone else crashes. We have to be the people willing to have honest, hard conversations together. The Bible speaks of iron sharpening iron; one other way to think about that is this: If you are in relationship with us and we don't ask you the hard questions, who will? We need one another to show compassion, care, and concern by helping each other maintain a healthy, vibrant, Kingdom perspective.

Perspective Is Robbed by Bad Systems and Bad Choices

Many of us have fallen into the trap of thinking our God-given purpose is simply a Christianized version of the American Dream. But following God requires Kingdom perspective, setting our eyes on things that are unseen, and stewarding well the things He has given us to steward, both tangible and intangible. Unfortunately, worldly systems can rob our eternal perspective if we aren't careful.

Entitlement and greed are rooted in many of our worldly systems, including banking, college, and even major business. Society teaches us that we are entitled to certain things, even when we can't actually afford them. Banks capitalize on that entitlement by creating loans that make us beholden to them for years of our lives. When you have systems in place that are unrighteous, it steals hope.

During the recession of 2007, a successful man came to Bob asking for money. He said, "I need $20,000 a month to carry my burden and I'd like you to help me."

"Twenty thousand dollars a month? Wow!" Bob said. Bob asked him a bunch of questions and it turned out this man had loans on a motor home, ski boat, and jet skis; they were all financed. He wanted to keep his inflated quality of life and was looking to Bob to help support something he had not really earned in the first place.

Bob felt the Spirit of the Lord come on him and he said, "I'm not going to help you out of your irresponsibility. Take the motor home, the ski boat, and the jet skis back."

The man refused. There was only one thing keeping him from changing his situation for the better: "That would be so embarrassing," he said to Bob.

The recession was incredibly divisive, and Bob recognized this. He didn't judge this man, but he knew that the man's perspective had become skewed. What happened to so many people is that the banks, in order to raise money, decided to give loans to people who couldn't pay for them. They introduced signature-only loans, making it easier for anyone to get a loan. The second the market turned, those loans became junk loans and many people lost everything.

Part of having Kingdom perspective is living within your means and working hard. This is a difficult one for people of faith because there are times when we push past our current situation by faith. The thing is, we can't live in the push. It is impossible to live long periods of time needing more income than you are earning. You cannot live your life with career goals but no practical steps to achieve them. At some point, you need to rebalance yourself and get perspective on where you are today.

There is a divine tension when we begin to discover that our career and path are ordained by God and that He prepared our lives before time began. The tension is that we start to get excited and sometimes look at the future as our hope versus living this day that God has made and rejoicing in what He is doing now. When our hope for what is coming is more exciting than our life now, we resort to escapism in our perspective, where we use our hope for the future as our motivator and we stop existing in the now.

Giving Up the God Card

Part of maturing in our perspective and purpose is letting go of (or loosely holding onto) the things God has shown us. We've already learned how being teachable is an important part of navigating our process with God. Teachability is also important when it comes to perspective. If we feel entitled to the things God is saying, then we tend to lose sight of what He is actually doing in our lives. This becomes our God card.

Shawn once had a contractor on a video game development team who believed he heard from God for a project for them to do. They were only working on contract work, so they were not developing their own projects. They had a deadline, and it was all work with no personal ambitions creatively. But this contractor had a lot of personal ambition and wanted to use the company to fulfill it.

They had a meeting where he presented, and Shawn gave him a clear no. Then he went above Shawn to the investment company that backed them, and they were taken off guard and told him, "No, thank you. Please don't talk to us again." He threw a fit because he felt like God had told him to do this, and Shawn's company had to let him go so he could go work on it. After the project did not amount to anything, the contractor wrote a note and wanted to come after the company legally because he felt his spiritual opinion was not validated.

There was no lawyer who would take the case: a contractor who had his own agenda was mad at the company he was contracting with because they wouldn't pay for his idea. It was so absurd, but that is what happens when entitlement enters our perspective. It's like a disease that lies to us.

Not all of our God cards are fueled by entitlement, but they still manipulate our perspective. We both have God cards, but we've learned how to hold them loosely. When you hold them tightly, you create plans around them, and you try to make them happen on your own.

Years ago, Shawn had the God card that he was supposed to be a senior pastor. Cherie challenged him one day and said, "Oh, you're not supposed to be a senior pastor anymore." This challenged Shawn's identity, and he said, "How dare you? This is who I am."

"Did God tell you that for the rest of your life you're going to be a senior pastor?" she asked.

"No."

"Well, how do you know this is still your role?"

Shawn went to a therapist, and he did the same thing. The therapist said, "This sounds exhausting for you. You're telling me all the things you want to do. They're all creative and inspiring people, and they take a lot of self-work, but pastoring takes a lot of community work where your life is focused on the people, not on your dreams. And you have dreams, so why would God give you dreams and not give you the ability, through a career, to manage those? I feel like you have this God statement inside of you that you can't violate because you're going to violate your connection to Him."

The God card shows up in many different ways. It can be dreams that we have but we aren't even working toward. It can be relationships that we think God is ordaining but we are not doing anything to pursue. In many cases, God did speak these things into our hearts, but we don't leave any room for God to interact with us regarding that topic.

The moment you believe in something so strongly that it leaves no room for modification or process is the moment that the Creator God, who comes in a million different ways, is limited to your imagination. This violates the ability for the miracle of faith to come into fullness. It violates our perspective of God, life, and opportunity.

One of the things that we're always trying to do is to be malleable: to shift and adjust, to be teachable, and to be available. If you are stuck, your perspective feels limited, or you are continually in a cycle of disappointment because God's former promises haven't come to pass, it may be time to lay down the God card. Invite people into your process, share God's words, and allow the question to be asked: That is what God said then, but what is God saying now?

Perspective and Your Marketplace Calling

The story of Joseph is one of the best biblical examples of how our perspective impacts our marketplace calling. As a young boy, Joseph was favored by his father, causing jealousy with his brothers. Then Joseph had a dream straight from heaven about how everyone in his family was going to bow down to him. His brothers took it as delusional and hated the attitude of his heart to the point where they planned his murder, but instead they threw him in a pit to be sold into slavery.

Joseph had a will to live, and in every circumstance—as a foreigner, slave, prisoner with a criminal record—he kept his perspective on who God is and who God called him to be. He grounded himself in truth and stayed the course of his internal convictions. Because of this, in each circumstance, he rose to a high place of service and influence.

It's important to know that it was fifty years between the time Joseph was sold into slavery and the moment he revealed himself to his brothers who came to Egypt needing help. Perseverance and Kingdom perspective allowed him to see the fruit of his calling.

In all of the biblical examples we've looked at so far—Daniel, Esther, Joseph, Solomon—they had more than just revelation, wisdom of the times and seasons, and confidence in their calling. They had perspective. And when they had endless hardship, they also had triumphant hope that God would deliver them and deliver their people.

When our process looks different from what we imagined (and it will!), perspective allows you to remain confident in your marketplace calling. Like Joseph, it helps you endure different seasons and unexpected changes, and most of all, it helps you keep your eyes on Jesus.

Balancing Spiritual and Natural Perspective

We must become fairly well rounded in the intersection of the practical and the Kingdom of heaven. We have been around Christian advisers who focus on metrics and a formula and not on God. We have also been around Christian advisers who avoid metrics and data and instead rely on dreams and hope, calling it faith.

Our perspective must be grounded in what God is showing us and also how to implement it. We need the metrics, and when they do not line up with faith, we need to press into that conflict until we hear God or can make a practical decision and not get stuck.

Shawn was in an Asian nation where a CEO of a large-parts manufacturing company had invited spiritual advisers to help problem solve some areas. He wanted to know if he was dealing with warfare or bad-intentioned people, because they were hitting problems with cash flow and growth that he couldn't figure out how to get past. One of the spiritual advisory-team members was also a businessman in a similar business, and he said, "Can I take a look at your financials?"

The CEO, however, explained that he wanted a spiritual answer for a spiritual issue and didn't seem to want to share any practical data. As the team prayed, they kept sensing that the CEO was the origin of many issues. Finally, his director said, "Let's show the P&L from last period." When they reviewed the metrics, a lot came to light: overspending, personally benefiting while the corporation was suffering, cash-outs of assets, even bribes for work. The problems were clear. The CEO was compromising his company, and God was either lifting His blessing or allowing this man to reap what he was sowing.

In the same week, Shawn went to another business to do some spiritual advising to the board and CEO. They had laid out all the practical data and were also stuck in some areas but extremely vulnerable. They were looking for practical solutions, but the area they were pioneering in the entertainment industry was extremely new for their country. They were like the tip of a spear going into an area that just hadn't been developed, and they were putting all their eggs in that basket. As Shawn advised them to diversify, he had a picture of a rival company that had split from their own and was trying to sabotage their relationships. They confirmed this and they began to pray blessing and release peace. There was such a turnaround because they addressed the spiritual issue. The former employee, who had founded the rival company, even called them to repent that same week and stopped the chain of gossip and lying that had been sabotaging the company.

Balanced perspective takes into account both the natural and the spiritual circumstances in life and our careers. When we are vulnerable to both perspectives, we are open to see how God is moving and how to bring the most connection to His Kingdom around us.

This process is different for everyone, but we all have one thing in common: we tend to avoid the conflict, especially in the natural, and hope that God just fixes it. This is the opposite of waiting on God. It is, rather, spiritual procrastination and will not lead to fruit.

When we do experience conflict, obstacles, or tension, particularly in business, it helps to see the big picture of what God wants to do. This perspective allows us to put the current tension in order of priority for how to tackle it. Other times, we see the big picture, but we need to be able to see the task list at hand and feel empowered that working hard through those details is what leads to big results, even when we feel lost in the details.

Part of what builds, and balances, perspective is being around someone who has a 30,000-foot perspective. Every organization needs a relationship with someone who can see the larger vision and build momentum toward that vision. We then need someone on the ground to see how to implement that large vision by breaking it into smaller tasks, like hacking through the jungle with a machete. If we are all on the ground with machetes, then no one will know where we are going. If we all live up in the air, then we won't ever get anything done.

We see the importance of a balanced perspective in the parable of talents. Each of the laborers had a different perspective when it came to the master's orders. The man who buried the talent did so out of fear. He believed the master to be a hard man.

The truth is, the master was willing for his workers to risk his money through investing. He understood what he was asking them to do, but out of fear and unbelief, the worker chose to limit his perspective and hide his talent.

The worker who gained the most return on his investment approached the master with a completely different perspective. He chose to honor the master's trust in him and do his very best with what he was given. It was this balanced perspective that brought about the greatest fruit. The worker approached his role with the heavenly perspective of "I am enough" and the natural perspective that careful investment would wield the greatest return.

Perspective takes faith. It requires knowing that God chose you and gave you an idea, dream, or calling. It also takes knowledge, under-standing, and wisdom—both from God and in the natural—to keep you moving forward and making progress on the thing He has called you to. When we lose this balance of perspective, we can easily fall back into our tightly gripped God cards.

Most importantly, we have to have an encounter with God's love and His heart to stay in the right perspective. Without Him, the moment we face challenges, we will lose sight of where we were headed.

Set Your Mind on Things Above

Man's sin is often obvious. Schemes and politics are often retold over and over, so information and dirt are everywhere. Satan is a knowledge broker and uses fear and threats to rule. As we build our perspective, we need to have discernment for people and for spiritual dynamics. At the same time, we need to "set [our] minds on things above, not on earthly things" (Colossians 3:2, NIV).

When you end up talking to someone who is not grounded in this passage, then they are typically grounded in information and, sometimes, in the worst cases, conspiracy. They know the secrets behind the scenes, but do they have a perspective for what God is doing, for what He wants to do? This is what can change the world. Knowing where the problems are, or even worse, getting caught up in conspiracy and focusing on this alone, creates fear, disconnect, and ultimately religion without relationship.

What does this mean practically? Well, we can look at Justin Bieber as an example. The religious sector of the church immediately started to blacklist him when he proclaimed salvation and used his Instagram to host prayer times with his followers. Why? Because they were holding him responsible for who he was before he became a Christian.

Perspective helps us to see where God has changed people, systems, and industries. It helps us to look past their immaturity, sin, and weakness and see what God values in them.

Shawn has a friend who bought into an agricultural industry that has one of the worst reputations in the world. People were mad at him for aligning with it. It made newspapers and people called him a sellout. He felt that God had shown him to buy it; it was actually a great investment because the industry was at an all-time low. Despite the negative perspectives, he maintained his sight on things above. He ended up bringing best practices into the industry of which he owned the majority. Then he turned it into organic farming, began to work on the soil, and gave incentives for other farms in the industry to build it back up the right way.

To this day, the anti-big-agriculture watch dog groups misunderstand much of the work he has done behind the scenes, but his product has made a comeback and God is blessing the integrity with which he is building. If you look at some of the reports online, you would think he is opportunistic, but if you saw the metrics, the changes, and the heart behind it, you would realize God put him on a rescue mission to restore this great product and agriculture, all because he chose to have a heavenly perspective.

How to Develop Perspective in the Marketplace

A healthy, heavenly perspective is so important on our journey in marketplace influence. Sometimes even practicing perspective for yourself or others can help you begin to shift your mindset to see people, circumstances, solutions, and career opportunities from God's perspective.

Here are three keys to building a new perspective:

1. Pray and ask God for His heart in a situation.
2. Look for what God is doing in that situation. In other words, look for the positive.
3. Look for the connection between your accomplishments, goals, and God's voice. This is the divine appointment.

ACTIVATION

Grab a long piece of paper and colored pencils and a ruler.

Draw a long line across the bottom of your paper, with plenty of room to write above it. You are creating a timeline. In the middle of your line, write today's date. On the left of your timeline, write every key milestone and accomplishment over a period of a year (or more, if you need to reach back a little bit). Make these bullet points. Try to make your timeline exhaustive. Ask co-workers, bosses, employees, and friends to help in order to make this an exhaustive list.

Take a different colored pen, and to the right of today's date, fill in your goals you have for your career, business, or employment for the next twelve months. For example, do you want to make more money? How many new clients do you want each month? Do you want to launch a new product, service, or department? Do you want to go after some venture capital? Are you doing a creative project and what is the timeline?

Now that all of that is done, compare your accomplishments in the past year to your business goals. Can you see where your accomplishments are moving you closer to your goals? What are you proud of? What are you hopeful for? What are the key ingredients that you can see will help you toward your goals? Are there any missing ingredients you need to add or is there something you should stop because it is not helping you in your forward pursuit?

Asking ourselves real questions by doing a self-check and putting it on paper can help bring new perspective for our marketplace role. Ultimately, perspective is a gift that God gives us as we draw close to Him in relationship to see our lives the way He does.

CHAPTER 10

Armor

We live in a very real conflict between two opposing kingdoms: the Kingdom of God and the kingdom of darkness.

The full armor of God is not just a Sunday school prayer and it is not just something to take into account on a Sunday morning. The enemy is *actively* scheming against us. He wants to wipe us out and we are in a real spiritual battle. We are not in a battle that is just fighting for our place in our space or industry. There is truly a massive heavenly war that impacts us in the spiritual and the natural realms. How do we battle and get breakthroughs?

> Put on God's complete set of armor provided for us, so that you will be protected as you fight against the evil strategies of the accuser! Your hand-to-hand combat is not with human beings, but with the highest principalities and authorities operating in rebellion under the heavenly realms. For they are a powerful class of demon-gods and evil spirits that hold this dark world in bondage. Because of this, you must wear all the armor

that God provides so you're protected as you confront the slanderer, for you are destined for all things and will rise victorious. Put on truth as a belt to strengthen you to stand in triumph. Put on holiness as the protective armor that covers your heart. Stand on your feet alert, then you will always be ready to share the blessings of peace. In every battle, take faith as your wrap-around shield, for it is able to extinguish the blazing arrows coming at you from the Evil One! Embrace the power of salvation's full deliverance, like a helmet to protect your thoughts from lies. And take the mighty razor-sharp Spirit-sword of the spoken Word of God. Pray passionately in the Spirit, as you constantly intercede with every form of prayer at all times. Pray the blessings of God upon all his believers. (Ephesians 6:11-18, TPT)

This is a serious commission to position our life in faith. We are in a battle and we need armor. There are so many things coming at us from the media, from co-workers, from extended family, from politics. God gave us armor so we could be protected from the worst this world and the enemy have to offer.

Having the armor of God and a sword of the Spirit as your protecting devices is not just cute sentimentality; it is actually a way of life. Setting up a prayer schedule and planning it just like you plan the most important meetings in your week are things that will help you thrive internally, no matter what good or hard thing is happening externally.

Not only are we standing against powers and principalities and rulers of the air, but we also must work with other humans who have very free will and who have their own agendas, their own sinful patterns, their own problems. These two issues fill our marketplace with odds that are stacked against us unless we have the hope of our relationship with Jesus to make a difference.

> For although we live in the natural realm, we do not wage a military campaign employing human weapons, using manipulation to achieve our aims. Instead, our spiritual weapons are energized with divine power to effectively dismantle the defenses behind which people hide. We can demolish every deceptive fantasy that opposes God and break through every arrogant attitude that is raised up in defiance of the true knowledge of God. We capture, like prisoners of war, every thought and insist that it bow in obedience to the Anointed One. Since we are armed with such dynamic weaponry, we stand ready to punish any trace of rebellion, as soon as you choose complete obedience. (2 Corinthians 10: 3-6, TPT)

Armed with Dynamic Weaponry

We fight the good fight by being connected to God and listening, obeying, standing, and believing. The Kingdom is a relational kingdom and so the armor and weapons we have are dynamic weaponry, meant to be partnered with relationship. When we talk about putting the full armor of God on, what is that for? It's for us to look to Jesus.

We want to highlight some of the dynamic weaponry that is available to you through your relationship with God. As you navigate the battles, both spiritual and tangible in your marketplace calling and in life, these are the spiritual weapons you can pull on as you partner with Jesus to see Him get His full reward.

The Word of God

The Bible does not give us direct career advice, but it does provide a framework to build our identities with the Kingdom mindset that we described earlier. It resets us and helps the Holy Spirit make us a new creation, and it renews our thinking. When we have the foundation of the Bible inside of us and begin to not just memorize but also apply the principles in our character, relationships, and choices, this is when it becomes a weapon.

Remember when Satan tried to seduce Jesus during the forty-day fast in the wilderness? He offered Jesus very tangible real-world power and influence, and Jesus answered each time with the words of Scripture, which He had meditated upon until it became life to Him.

Recently, one of Bob's employees accused another of a specific HR concern. Bob's team heard them both out and the one who was being accused carried an inner confidence. Although he looked weary, he had an inner strength. Bob said to him, "I feel so much strength in you. Where is it coming from?" The employee said, "I keep meditating on Psalm 138:8: 'The Lord will vindicate me. Your love, Lord, endures forever—do not abandon the works of your hand.' And I get confidence because I do not feel like I have done anything wrong."

The other employee had built quite a case, but when the team went through it, they realized there was nothing there. The HR concern was more of a jumbled mess of the first employee's poor boundaries and expectations. The second employee thanked Bob and the team at the end but did not feel shaken by it or the process. He just kept being himself.

Later, they found out the first employee had not been fulfilling many of his responsibilities and they had to let him go. The second employee felt vindicated because he was constantly bringing his best to the table and did not complain, and the one who brought his worst to the table and accused others was no longer even in the company. It was like the Bible was playing out before him and it built so much of his spiritual testimony of who God is to him.

It is also the words that God speaks directly to our hearts that we carry with us into battle. Back in the mid-eighties, Bob's wife, Lauren, had a strong encounter from the Lord to buy a piece of land that they could not afford. But they bought it anyway because it was so clearly a directive from God.

At one point, that piece of land became a battlefield. The city tried to take it to use for the fire department, claiming eminent domain, and Bob and Lauren had to go into a very intense petition for their land. Lauren had heard from God so clearly that she had a level of fight in her that only a word from God can energize. Lauren and Bob went together, and she stood up to the fire council and told them that it was the Lord's land and what her plans were and all the scriptures to back it up. They fought for the provision knowing they had God's right to it. Lauren preached to the whole fire council, and when she was done, they said, "Mr. Hasson, do you have anything to say?" And Bob said, "Nope." They said, "Obviously you're a smart man," and they voted, and they did not take the land by eminent domain.

Many promises from God, business ventures, resources that we try to obtain, and other things God brings into our lives can create a battle, but it's worth it! Having the Word and the Spirit speaking to us will cause us to keep emerging in His victory over and over in our process. When we hear God, we can stand with a different measure of faith. God's Word empowers us to hope for things to happen when there are no natural indicators of them happening. We are also able to martial our energy not on the conflict or conspiracy or breakdown we are experiencing but on applying faith to our circumstance.

God's Promise to Use All Things for Our Good

We have this incredible promise from God in Romans 8:28 that He will use all things for our good, which becomes a weapon for us when we are going through the worst. We love what Christine Caine says: "When you are going through hell, keep going!" God will take our problems and bring solutions that are not even an option today. He will take negotiations or mediations and provide options that are not on the table. He also has long-term sight and is working toward lifelong goals with us.

We often hear success coaches say, "It's not a problem. It's an opportunity," which is true, but it demeans the depth of what we are going through. It might be an opportunity, but it is a problem. At the end of the day, we must learn how to go through it and apply our faith and grow.

When Shawn worked in the video game industry, one of the main video game contracts was pulled right at the end of development. Both the client and the contractor pulled out and all the finances were gone and the rights to the game were taken as well. The hiring company needed a write-off and the contractor didn't want to take the risk to help distribute it because they had experienced a bad year and needed only triple-A titles if they were going to go forward. It felt like a huge loss—Shawn and his team had spent two years of their lives on that game. The morale was so low. At the time, they weren't aware that 60 percent of video games were canceled at that stage in development. Shawn went to God and asked Him why that happened. All that he heard was Romans 8:28.

Through that game, the company developed many relationships in the entertainment industry. Despite the canceled contract, those connections opened the doors to many opportunities for the next four years that Shawn and his team wouldn't have had without it.

The process also led Shawn to identify that he didn't want to be primarily in the video game industry—it wasn't his primary purpose or career path. Had the game succeeded, he probably would have stayed in the industry longer than he should have. Instead, he allowed Romans 8:28 to be in his heart, and God used the failure of that project to keep him grounded in his true passion and calling.

Forgiveness

A consulting client of Shawn's had a contract with a believer who ultimately failed to fulfill the contract. When Shawn's client learned that the end product was very successful, but his contract remained unpaid, he wasn't sure what to do. His lawyer told him to take the other business to court. However, Shawn's client did not want to ruin the other company or its owners with a lawsuit. He decided to speak to his pastor about the issue instead.

His pastor's first reaction was to say, "Let's pray." And they did. "You can get this money and you'll win," the pastor said, "but it's going to tie you up for two to five years and then there's going to be bad reputations on both sides for a long time, and you're just going to be exhausted. It's going to take some of your best energy and be exhausting." And then he said, "In my spirit I see you letting this go, knowing that you're going to reproduce like this again in your lifetime several times, but this is the last time for this person. You could let them go, let them be with God, let this amount go and honor God for that. You can say to God that you're responsible for this debt for them, and release this to Him knowing in faith, believing in faith, that you'll make money again."

As the pastor spoke, the client knew it was from God, and he decided to burn the contract. Shawn's client ended up forgiving the debt and moving forward in his career. Years later, he was called by the new managers of the company that hadn't paid him and they asked for him to work for them again. He did, and he received tons of new business from that arrangement and saw how God redeems in the long term. He realized that God creates all kinds of opportunity if we forgive.

How is forgiveness dynamic weaponry? It's weaponry because the world's systems emphasize right and wrong and retribution, but forgiveness is the Kingdom's weapon of redemption. When we choose forgiveness as our weapon, we recognize that God will redeem what was lost and that He wants to not only redeem our loss but also salvage the lives, time, and families of both parties. In the end, forgiveness releases us from getting entangled in the world's idea of justice and gives us the freedom to move forward.

Integrity

Integrity is a key characteristic of the Father that we are meant to reflect. When we are armed with dynamic integrity, however, it becomes a weapon in situations that would challenge the core of who we are. Every single day our integrity is at stake. And we must ask ourselves, are we going to do the right thing?

A friend of Shawn's is the chief of staff for a prestigious hospital. Right before the position became available, however, he got a malpractice suit filed against him. He found out that the suit was filed by a relative of his competitor for the chief of staff position. They had purposefully filed the suit so that it would take him out of the running for the job.

He and Shawn prayed together, and he asked, "What should I do? I know that this is a distant relative, I can prove it, but by the time we prove it, he'll already have the job. This is so unjust."

Shawn asked him what he really wanted in that situation. "I want this position," he said. "I've fought my whole life for this position, and I want the leadership role."

"Okay," Shawn replied, "I want you to surrender that to God." He explained the importance of surrendering the desire to God and allowing God to take control of the situation. Shawn recognized that if his friend tried to justify himself and prove the other candidate's lack of integrity, it could end up ruining his own career and integrity in the process. So they prayed.

In the end, the other doctor got the job, rather than Shawn's friend. Years later, however, he received a call from the hospital where he had originally trained about coming on as their chief of staff. It was near his wife's hometown and it was a hospital he loved. "We know you're not here," the hospital administrator said to him over the phone, "and we have people here who could do it, but we heard you were up for another position and we know all about the scenario at your current hospital. You have integrity and we need a man like you to lead this, and the Board of Directors wants you."

Shawn's friend was handed his dream position because of his integrity. They had watched him navigate working for a hospital administrator who had unjustly taken his position while staying true to his heart and serving his patients and community. Instead of fighting injustice with injustice, he let integrity be his weapon of choice.

Hope and the Ability to Marshal Our Energy Wisely

Another incredibly dynamic weapon we have is the hope of our future calling. We are in this life for the long haul and it leads to our everlasting life with Jesus. That means that while we work in our present situations with integrity and grace, we do not have to hold onto it as though it is our only chance at our calling.

One of the fruits of the Spirit in Galatians 5:23 (MSG) is described this way: "We find ourselves involved in loyal commitments, not needing to force our way in life, able to marshal and direct our energies wisely."

This is exactly one of the things that happens when we are rooted in faith and hope and walking in sync with the Spirit of God. Many people are overtaxed and overburdened and can't slow down to rest. They are accustomed to running over colleagues in pursuit of better opportunities.

When we follow God's process, however, and stand firm in the Word, despite our circumstances, we do not have to force our way into our callings or career opportunities. We can rest in hope and in the knowledge of God's will, trust Him, and choose wisely how to direct our energy.

Bob was once in a meeting to discuss a possible business contract. The other business owner told him, "Son, this is all I am offering and all I have for the job. You have a business decision to make." And Bob looked at him and said, "I don't understand. You're asking me to take this job for less than what we agreed."

"Yeah, that's a business decision," the man replied. "You must decide: is it worth it in the short-term to put a deal together so that you can end up (A) staying in business, and (B) doing business with me in the long term? That's a business decision."

Bob took the job, even though everything in him was telling him to fight, fight, fight! He ended up doing business with that same company for over thirty years. They are one of his longest-standing customers. At the outset, he had to take a cut and work hard on a job that may or may not have paid off. But Bob had hope for the future and knew that God would show him how to marshal his energy wisely. If it was not the right fit, he would be able to move on after that first difficult job. Instead, he ended up earning a loyal customer throughout his career and a valuable understanding of where to put his energy in business.

Boundaries

One of the main weapons and defenses we have in warfare is to have clear boundaries professionally, personally, and spiritually. You can tell when you have been in business long enough if the group you want to contract with has their systems—or boundaries—in place.

We see the importance of boundaries in Nehemiah 4, when the people of Judah rebuilt Jerusalem. As they began rebuilding the wall, the enemy plotted against them because the wall would prevent them from accessing the city. The people of Judah had to divide up and build the wall with weapons at their sides and others protecting them as they built. The guards and their weapons served as their boundaries, their strategy for protection, even as they built a physical boundary around their city.

God is our strength and shield, but we have to also implement this virtue of boundaries in the natural. As people of the marketplace, we can do this by setting up great structure, good communication, a legal team, healthy HR processes, the right accounting, etc. Maybe these aren't the areas where you need to build your "wall," but they are examples of having the structure around you that will hold you when the enemy comes.

Boundaries are a dynamic weapon that allow us to establish a strategy of defense in the broken systems that make up many of the marketplace industries. They protect us from unexpected decisions, broken contracts, and unpaid bills. In relationship, boundaries help us set clear expectations and healthy communication. Instead of depending on the broken systems of your industry, work with God to set up incredible boundaries and healthy self-management so that your career or business can flourish.

The Full Armor of God

Every piece of our dynamic weaponry is meant to be used through relationship with God. As we learn to implement this weaponry in our daily lives and in our careers, we actually reflect God to those around us. We look more like Jesus.

We often equate warfare and weaponry with fighting other people who oppose us, but that is the world's view of warfare. The armor of God is a spiritual truth that plays out in our treatment of others, the way we navigate difficult situations, the choices we make, and the way we present God and His Kingdom to the world. It is powerful and effective, and it is meant to protect us from the enemy while also bringing us and others closer to God.

The armor of God is a powerful resource that is readily available. You have been given these dynamic weapons to help you in your marketplace calling and it is time to put them to good use.

ACTIVATION

1. What part of Ephesians 6:11-18 do you use regularly?
2. What is a dynamic weapon you have been given and use regularly?
3. What are you doing today to grow in your integrity?
4. What are healthy boundaries you can have at work and at home?

CHAPTER 11

Prosper

God is a father, and a father's nature is to provide for his family. Everything we truly need, before we even think of it, God has resourced for us. As a matter of fact, for every destiny God created us with, there is a plan of full provision accompanying it.

Provision on its own is never the vision or the end goal. Rather, provision is His resource provided so that we can walk out His will and love, reach, and develop the people to whom God has called us.

We see God demonstrate this with the Israelites in multiple ways all throughout the Old Testament. The two most notable ways we want to focus on come from Deuteronomy and Exodus.

> But remember the Lord your God, for it is he who gives
> you the ability to produce wealth, and so confirms his
> covenant, which he swore to your ancestors, as it is today.
> (Deuteronomy 8:18, NIV)

God is saying that the ability to produce resource and wealth comes from Him, and it is linked to His nature over His chosen people. We need to know that He is our rock and refuge and that all resources flow out of His great love for us.

In Exodus 31, God anointed Bezalel to be able to have the creativity, artistic ability, and skill to create a place of worship with all the resources that God was bringing Israel:

> Then the Lord said to Moses, "See, I have chosen Bezalel son of Uri, the son of Hur, of the tribe of Judah, and I have filled him with the Spirit of God, with wisdom, with understanding, with knowledge and with all kinds of skills." (Exodus 31:1-3, NIV)

God is in the business of providing resources for all our purposes. As all the tribe of Judah watched, God poured out His favor and destiny on Bezalel as he was chosen to display wisdom, understanding, knowledge, and skills. We are convinced that prior to Bezalel being anointed, he was an ordinary man, and the people of Judah were amazed at the favor poured out on him.

For every vision there is a provision. Resources, prosperity, and money are not the destiny of God's people, although they are part of our benefit. When we start to see what God has in store for those who love Him, it is not wealth or resources; it is walking in full connection with Him, ourselves, and the world around us. He provides so that we can live fully, much as a parent provides so that their children can fully develop. Walking in connection with Him is the resource and benefit behind the outward blessing of provision.

Learning to Receive

Matthew 5:8 says, "You're blessed when you get your inside world—your mind and heart—put right. Then you can see God in the outside world."

We must learn how to be receivers. Salvation is God's gift that we can't earn, and many Christians are workaholics for a grace they have already been given. They can't see the blessing because their inside world has not been put right. Human beings have a hard time receiving for many reasons, all of which we need to take to the cross. As Christians, our giving will not be out of the right motivation if we don't know how to receive from our Father.

Bob wrote in *Business of Honor* a story of his difficulty receiving gifts, primarily due to the shame that ruled his life. His wife, Lauren, loves to give him gifts, and in the past he has had a difficult time receiving them. Early in their marriage she surprised him with an expensive gift that she knew he wanted. When she gave it to him, he had this visceral reaction of unworthiness because he felt he didn't earn it. He was mad that she did it because he had wanted to work hard to earn it. It ended up being a marker in their lives of the Lord really uncovering Bob's need to learn how to receive.

Our basic desire to want to earn or accomplish can short-circuit God's ability to give us resources and talent we don't deserve. It's really one of the biggest struggles of walking in faith toward resources because we won't take opportunities, gifts, grants, or benefits that we don't feel like we earned.

This gift became a parable to Bob. It started him on the path of recognizing that God did not want to give him a stone if he asked for a fish. He did, however, want to give Bob every good and perfect gift, including his family. For over thirty years of marriage, as Lauren continues to give Bob things, he is learning to receive them as a loved son of God.

Sometimes we don't even feel worth being resourced, and this is a deep identity question that God wants to answer inside of us through Jesus. Even people in a successful thirty-year career are sometimes trapped in this mindset. If we are only looking at resources as a reward from God and not what God has planned from the beginning to resource us as His children, then we will be disappointed. We can't gain in our own strength what God has wired our expectation for spiritually.

This is where a lot of unworthiness comes from. We ask, "Am I worth it?" And we measure if something is right for us based on our own performance and not on the grace of God. We have the ultimate King as our Father, and so many of us are still trying to perform for resources that are important to us, resources that are so small in His Kingdom compared to what He has available.

Other times, people feel shame for some resource God has given them because they did not earn it. When this is our experience, we need to reevaluate our identity in Christ. We must choose to live in the big picture: the resources are for Him, His Kingdom, and His glory. Ultimately, when we are ashamed of a gift or provision that someone has given us, we are communicating that we are either unworthy or ashamed of them.

One of our friends was working as an assistant to the director (AD) on several commercials. He felt like God was going to bless him and give him favor in this new company, but he didn't expect the level of blessing he ended up receiving. His bosses kept on trying to give him more responsibility. They could see the potential in him, but he kept shrugging it off and not making it easy for them.

Eventually, they just let him run his course as an AD and he left the company discouraged. A few years later, his former boss approached him at a benefit and said, "Did you ever become a director?"

"Not yet," he replied, "but I am trying!"

"I wish you had let us help mentor you into it," his boss said. "We tried to give you director responsibilities because we could see your talent and wanted to grow you in that way, but you didn't seem to want it."

Our friend felt a sword pierce his heart. His own insecurity had short-circuited an opportunity he didn't even know was available. God was showing him something through the experience, and he worked on any sense of unworthiness or inability to receive that would stand in his way.

If God gives us something, we shouldn't be ashamed or feel guilty about it, but we need to use it as a tool to receive and give love. In other words, when we see resource coming from a Father who loves us, we won't just sell it or give it away when we are supposed to inherit it. Like Esau giving up his inheritance for a bowl of soup, there are times we are tempted to be "normal" or to shun God's extravagance because of other needs in our lives or the needs of others. But if we have a relationship with God as Father, we know that we cannot just cast off the resource that He has provided; it is meant to be used for our calling and for His Kingdom.

Prosperity Is Not a Divine Right, But We Do Get Blessed

For the sake of some of you reading this, we need to make sure to distinguish the message of provision from the hyper-wealth message of our day.

When false teachers say that extreme prosperity is the divine right of every Christian, there is the danger that we will neglect the comforting truth that God does provide, not just the minimum, but as Paul expresses it, "Exceedingly abundantly above all that we ask or think" (Ephesians 3:20, NKJV)—or in the Passion Translation: "God can do anything, you know—far more than you could ever imagine or guess or request in your wildest dreams! He does it not by pushing us around but by working within us, his Spirit deeply and gently within us."

Whenever there is a false teaching, there is the danger that we will overreact by neglecting the true doctrine. This excerpt from *The Ways of Prosperity*, by Jeremy and Ally Butrous, helps unpack the difference between the hyper-wealth message and Kingdom prosperity:

We believe it is time for the misleading and limiting "prosperity gospel" message to be abolished. True prosperity is so much more. In essence it is a life in which we partner with Jesus. It is journeying with Him in intimate, loving, powerful, and purposeful ways. In this context, money is viewed simply as a tool to maximize our opportunity to display the will of the Father.

Sadly, tradition and culture have presented us with a minimalist perspective on the ways God wants to prosper us. It is easy for us to miss the depth of God's goodness in all the facets and avenues of His love. God wants to be our ultimate provider. He wants us to partner with the supernatural and natural ways of provision. . . . Through this process, God will be more deeply revealed as the ultimate life source of good, the ultimate provider, the ultimate King. (*The Ways of Prosperity*, p. viii)

We do not have a "divine right" to extreme prosperity, as some have falsely taught. But neither do we need to feel guilty about the material things God provides for us. Of course, we need to hold everything before God; the resources we have are His, and through Him we get to steward them as sons and daughters. Paul even reminded Timothy to help people "[to] be generous and ready to share" (1 Timothy 6:18), storing up treasure in heaven. But when God blesses us materially, we can thankfully enjoy the things He has richly supplied.

The Bible is full of examples of God's abundant provision for His people, whether it was for taxes—Matthew 17:27: "But so that we may not cause offense, go to the lake and throw out your line. Take the first fish you catch; open its mouth and you will find a four-drachma coin. Take it and give it to them for my tax and yours."—or the donkey the Father provided for Jesus to ride on to fulfill prophetic scripture in Matthew 21:2-3, saying to them, "Go to the village ahead of you, and at once you will find a donkey tied there, with her colt by her. Untie them and bring them to me. If anyone says anything to you, say that the Lord needs them, and he will send them right away."

As we navigate these wealth messages, whether they are more extreme or more balanced, it helps to weigh our understanding of provision and prosperity against this: Do you need this resource to bring Jesus His reward and fulfill your destiny of loving the people He is calling you to?

While radical wealth is not our divine right, God is in the business of providing. And if that is our Father's business, then it should be ours as well. Provision isn't about hoarding wealth. When you begin to see God as a provider and that provision comes from His Father heart, then you also become a provider on the earth. You come not just to receive but also to give.

Provision Requires Faith

Part of the way we access this bountiful heart of God is to really hear Him and walk in faith.

Several years ago, Bob and his wife, Lauren, learned how God weaves together His resources for everything He has appointed in our lives. We mentioned previously how Lauren had a strong encounter with the Lord in the mid-eighties to buy a piece of land that they could not afford. But they bought it anyway because it was so clearly a directive from God.

For twenty years, they held onto the land, not knowing its purpose. During those twenty years, they ended up going through a rough business cycle and were on the verge of losing everything. They looked through all their personal assets and decided to have the land appraised. It had appreciated so much that it was able to collateralize a multimillion-dollar loan they needed for the company to establish cashflow. They were amazed at God. That act of obedience early on helped them dig out of that season and they hit some success and paid that loan off. Then the land became clear to build on again and they were able to build the home that they are in now.

Bob had always hoped they could sell the lot and get the cash, but since Lauren had heard God so clearly, she drew a line in the sand. The lot went from providing for their business at a time when they would have been out of business to being a place where they could build a home not only for their family but also for all the people to whom Bob and Lauren minister.

Every promise comes with a process, and part of that process is apprehending the resources that it takes to accomplish the promise. It's good to make a plan to accomplish our five-year goals. However, we also need to look at the greater works God is leading us to believe for and begin to dream, pray, and strategize with God.

Thriving in the marketplace requires faith. Without it, we end up operating out of our human strength, which leads to the survival of the fittest. We may accomplish a lot of things on our own strength, but the price is high and often devastating. We haven't met many people who are self-made who haven't also suffered huge consequences in some area of their lives.

When you let God father you and show you by His Spirit what is in store for your life, you begin to tap into true provision, which is the untold riches of His heart. God brings provision in abundance for all our needs. As we said before, God's primary nature is first a Father. Jesus even compares Him to natural fathers on Earth, saying in Matthew 6:25-26 (TPT):

This is why I tell you to never be worried about your life, for all that you need will be provided, such as food, water, clothing—everything your body needs. Isn't there more to your life than a meal? Isn't your body more than clothing? Look at all the birds—do you think they worry about their existence? They don't plant or reap or store up food, yet your heavenly Father provides them each with food. Aren't you much more valuable to your Father than they?

God isn't just creative in His solutions and provision for our career goals and organizations; He also provides authority to move laws, rewrite systems, and be innovative. God created our life and even our dreams, and He knows we need resources to live them out. We also need to know Him as the one who provides. *Jehovah Jireh* (the Lord will provide) is not just a buzz word or a nice name; it is part of His nature that we can access. He will abundantly provide for all our needs—material, emotional, and spiritual.

In working with impoverished people for many years, we have watched God time and time again bring provision as one of the first acts of His love put on display in their lives. In Ecuador, we work with a nonprofit called Casa Mis Suenos, which reaches out to women in the red-light district and fights against human trafficking. They also help to rehabilitate women so they can start a new career. Our leaders of the organization were helping women out of prostitution but were shocked by the lack of resources, advocacy, and actual laws that would cover those—especially the minors—who were forced into sex trafficking. They were praying to God asking for breakthrough and finances because the laws and government policy were so hard to work with.

Then God showed one of the leaders that He was giving her the ability to not just help the women at risk but also to change the policy that the government uses when dealing with women coming out of trafficking. She wanted to make sure that these women and girls coming out of prostitution and trafficking would not have criminal records that would interfere with them being a productive career person in society. She didn't have a degree and had never written policy, but God provided a strategy, language, and connections, and within months she was before the president and government proposing anti-human trafficking legislation. It was passed unanimously and is now being followed.

Begin processing your resource needs with God, whether it is resources you have been given that you aren't sure what to do with or the resources required to accomplish a dream. Faith is active and expects our involvement. Begin processing things such as "I'm going to need these kinds of contracts, this kind of social capital, this kind of marketing, or this kind of finances" in order to accomplish this promise. If you're waiting on resources, planning for the future, or holding onto provision from God, bring that to God in prayer, knowing that He wants to partner with you to bring the resources you need.

Become a Provider

When Shawn and Cherie first moved to Los Angeles, it was in the middle of the recession of 2007. Not only that, but there was also an entertainment strike that put the entertainment industry in peril. Most of their congregation worked in the entertainment industry or were transplants to L.A.

One night, in the midst of experiencing what seemed like endless need, God spoke to Shawn as he cried out for the church, city, and nation:

"You don't need Me to come and just rescue you. You need Me to help change the culture of your mind and heart. You don't need a provider right now; I have given you the ability to produce resources in the hardest places on Earth. Everyone comes to L.A. to get something—a career, fame, education—but I have commissioned you to give something. You are called to be benefactors and release finances and resources."

Shawn and Cherie were struggling to pay the rent on their building and he was struggling to make it month to month even in his personal bills. But this changed everything. They repented of wanting an angel investor to come rescue them or any human being to just bail them out. They began to take on their rightful Kingdom mindset that just as the Father is a provider and benefactor and way maker, so too that is who they were supposed to be. We are supposed to do what we see the Father doing.

A friend of Shawn's, in that same season, had him read all the parables and said, "What if you represent the Father in these stories—like the parable of the lost son who squanders everything and the jealous brother. What if you are not supposed to see yourself as one or the other but as the father who gives the inheritance to the prodigal and who nurtures the jealous brother's heart, helping him to understand?"

That changed everything! As a church, as a leadership team, and individually, Shawn began to see himself as someone who could be a resource, not just someone who needed resources. That is who God is and that is who He wants to make you.

It started small at first. They gave a single mother some groceries one month. Then they paid for her daycare for a month and gave her more groceries. That was not rare for Shawn in life, but in the recession season it felt almost stupid to take what little he had and share it with someone. That second month, a film crew came and asked if they could use

Shawn and Cherie's rental house for a project for an independent film. The owner said, "Have them rent it and you keep the money. I want you blessed." They paid Shawn enough for the rest of their time in that house.

Each time we take on the nature of Jehovah Jireh, we begin to see both sides of provision: the need fulfilled and becoming like Him to fulfill the need for others.

Jesus Is Our Reward

When Jesus is the focus of our life, that means that when provision comes, we are balancing our perspective with Jesus in the center of view. We ask ourselves, is this resource for me, for my marriage, for my family, for my church, for my city, for my business? How is this part of the story of how my life gets to bring His transformative nature to the earth?

The Jewish people have been saying prayers about blessing and provision since time immemorial. Some prayers are even said weekly, like Numbers 6:24-26 (NIV): "The Lord bless you and keep you; the Lord make his face shine on you and be gracious to you; the Lord turn his face toward you and give you peace."

This prayer is all about receiving the expected blessing, favor, abundance, provision, social connections, and material blessings of God. God always sets His peoples' expectation that He would provide for them in unusual ways to show that He loves them—thus proving His nature to the world around them.

We see how provision and blessing were witnesses to the world in Solomon's life. The Queen of Sheba came to Solomon and saw all that he had built with the wisdom and abundance of God and said to him, "Surely your God loves His people because He has raised up a man like you! Praise be to your God!" (1 Kings 10:9, paraphrase). She worshiped God because she realized there was a drastic difference in her leadership and his. She was radically altered by the display of God's love and blessing on His people.

God's ultimate goal is always spiritual provision that brings transformation. When God brings a material, relational, business, or other type of blessing, He always has a spiritual reason behind it. There are even spiritual reasons if He withholds anything from us.

Stones of Remembrance

When you are learning to partner with God for resources, you need to look at the ongoing story that is already happening in your life as a prototype or example of how He can appear in your tomorrow. What does this mean? Consider the skills or talents, spiritual blessing, or meaningful relationships in your life. Were there moments when you got connected with someone who could encourage your career? Have you ever received gifts, opportunities, or trainings that pushed you toward a specific goal or talent? These are all ways to look for the thread of the Father providing for the assignment on your life.

Keep a journal or notebook with you, or on your phone, where you can track the moments of favor, increase, and financial breakthrough that you experience. When you're needing to believe for more or be encouraged by what God has already done, look back on your journal and remind yourself of all the ways God has provided. Invite Him to create a miracle again, but this time you can partner your faith to His provision, because He's done it before.

For Shawn, one of the divine symbols that God has used to remind him of His provision is watches. It started with a Rolex that he wrote about in *Keys to Heaven's Economy*. He ended up giving that Rolex away by the prompting of the Holy Spirit and it brought breakthrough to someone remarkably close to his heart. He thought, in a way, he would get an upgrade because, in his mind, it was about the value of the watch. You can't out-give God, right? Lots of times we are looking for a monetary reward for an obedient act.

Over the years, he continued to have a few more watch stories (not extravagant watches but all were meaningful), and he was wearing one of those watches on a ministry trip to South Korea. At that time, Shawn and Cherie's finances were tight, as they had been for many years. All of the opportunities they had for success felt way off for so long that they were just steady as she goes with hope for a breakthrough but not currently strong in faith.

While on the trip, a businessman asked his pastor if he could drive Shawn back to the hotel. Shawn hadn't met him before, but when they got into his amazing car, the businessman said, "I have to ask you something. Can I have your watch?"

That particular watch had been one of the gifts someone had given to Shawn, so he almost said no. When Shawn received the watch a few years before, it had represented that his season was changing into family and had been a confirmation that marriage was approaching. When you learn to interpret the signs and symbols, they keep coming.

However, Shawn felt prompted to give him the watch. The businessman said, "I am going to exchange it with mine and I have a prophetic word for you. Your season is changing and there is a new time of watching with the Lord. You will be getting up at a different hour to spend time with God and He will speak to you in new ways. Also, all of your finances from this time on are going to change and you will have enough for all your projects that God is calling you to pursue."

He put the watch on Shawn. It was a very expensive watch. "I bought that watch as a sign the day I had my biggest business breakthrough, and I know it's now your breakthrough."

Shawn was truly humbled and had no idea what to say. The next year they had such a change in their finances. They set some goals and changed the structure of their lives. Shawn released a successful book, *Translating God*, and they worked on huge financial planning for their lives. They also had another baby during that time, and Shawn would often do a night shift feeding her and would spend time just praying and loving her and Jesus. It was such a gift. Many of the prophetic words that connected Shawn to marketplace leaders happened in those late-night shifts.

The Jewish people in the Bible would pile stones of remembrance not only for themselves but also for their families and their tribes. They would place the stones where God had come through for them and they would go back to visit to remind themselves of the stories and the impact God had on them and previous generations.

> And each one of you take up a stone on his shoulder, according to the number of the tribes of the children of Israel, that this may be a sign among you when your children ask in time to come, saying, "What do these stones mean to you?" Then you shall answer them that the waters of the Jordan were cut off before the ark of the covenant of the Lord; when it crossed over the Jordan, the waters of the Jordan were cut off. And these stones shall be for a memorial to the children of Israel forever. (Joshua 4:5-7, NKJV)

Building stones of remembrance in our own lives is a prophetic act. Our stones of remembrance don't have to be items, watches, or even tangible things. Just keeping a journal and remembrance in your heart can bolster your faith.

God Speaks Through Provision

Learning to listen to God about our resources is so important and it's one of the primary training grounds for Kingdom living. Jesus talked about money over twenty-five times in the Gospels, and eleven out of thirty-nine parables were about money. Finances, resources, ownership areas, business, contracts—all of these practical, real-world things create a space for us to learn very quickly how to hear from God and recognize His provision.

In our Christian walk, when we are first learning how to hear from God, we read the Bible and learn how to apply it to our lives. Then we learn about conviction of sin, allow the Holy Spirit to show us areas that are falling short, and let Him rebuild us with His character. The final area, and one where many Christians struggle, is learning how to hear God's heart for provision and resources. Shawn's book *Provision* touches further on this topic and unpacks prayers, declarations, and prophecies to help believers understand God's provision.

What dreams are you dreaming that require huge resources? What roles and places of influence is God calling you to that don't seem feasible in your current situation? As you step out further in your marketplace role or calling, it's time to apply direct faith to your knowledge and understanding of who God is as Father and Provider. It's time to hear what He is saying about provision and resources to bring transformation to your career, life, city, and nation, starting today.

ACTIVATION

1. Create a list of resources that God is currently providing for you.
2. For each item in your list, ask Him how you can use those resources to advance.

CHAPTER 12

Fear regret more than failure—history has shown that we fail far more from timidity than we do from over daring. Or to quote a little Latin: Fortes fortuna adiuvat *(Fortune favors the bold).*

Margie Warrell

Most Christians can quote grandiose themes of scripture like "It's impossible to please God without faith!" But faith is fleshed out in our ability to take great risks. We have talked about building with God in the way we hear Him, including in our instinct and intuition. We have gone over the differences in our process compared to those who do not walk out a Christ-filled life. We have even written about some of the battles we will all face at times and the weapons that we have available. Now is where the proverbial rubber hits the road. There is no way to walk out a journey of listening to God without taking great risks in our careers and choices.

Holy Spirit Risk Assessment

God wants us to use every tool at our disposal, including our intellect and our life experience. Those can, of course, hinder us as well, but as people who are trying to take huge steps of faith, we should trust the tools available to us more than we are worried about them getting in the way. Remember, you have the mind of Christ. You are hardwired to hear His voice and you are capable of making great decisions. Our intellect and life experience are part of what makes us, us.

We must let God's Spirit disciple our minds and stay focused on what God can do for us, instead of focusing on how man will fail, what the economy might do, or what our competitors are planning.

Risk assessment and management in the world's system start with over-estimation of the probability of something going wrong. That means that people are using data to indicate if some of the biggest risks are worth it. The data never measure possibilities of changes unless they just predict current trends. Data did not predict Uber, Amazon, Netflix, or Google. Instead, they emerged out of great risk from the garages of people who weren't afraid to try something that hadn't been done before.

Not all risks have to have this high of stakes, but when we assess risks, we have to start with data, then measure the data against our internal compass and instinct. What is God saying? If you cannot hear Him directly, take a moment to imagine the God of the universe. He is the one who created this world with original ideas for industry, science, the medical field, agriculture, and so on. Is the field you are working in ready for a God installment of His original plan?

Imagine what God wants in your field. Think about the technologies that are missing, the economic injustices that need to be corrected, the manpower that needs to come. What would your job, business, or industry look like in its fullness? What would your opportunities look like if God were on the earth right now appointing you to this role? We do not have to be so super-spiritual to think we have to hear an audible voice in order to take risk, but we do need to process with spiritual intelligence and weigh some bigger variables than traditional risk management teaches us.

When Shawn and Cherie started their ministry and business, they needed office space and they also needed a home office. In Los Angeles, that is quite a feat for new organizations. An extra room in a house can add thousands to a rental price, and an office space for a budding team can run between five and ten thousand dollars per month. Shawn and Cherie had also received some prophetic words about saving for a house purchase and these three goals didn't seem to go together, but they prayed and stayed open.

At one point they received such a specific word about a house that Cherie actually found a physical listing that matched the word and supported the other words. It was a live/work property with both commercial and residential space. The problem was the price and the fact that it was a hot property and was receiving many offers. Shawn and Cherie didn't qualify, but they decided to take a risk and walk the word out in faith. They sent in an offer and wrote a letter asking the owner to help them, saying, "Sir, we need a miracle." The owner was shocked because the property was one of the only miracles that had ever come in his life. His grandmother had prophesied to him when he was young that he would move to America and receive a miracle property, and when it was time to pass it on, to do so to someone else who needed a miracle. Shawn and Cherie were given a chance to get the house, and it all worked out both naturally and supernaturally.

The greatest opportunities come to those who stay open to obedience in places that their own skill, talent, or network can't bring them. Faith is when you aren't a self-made man or woman, and you don't limit yourself to your own ability, but you trust that God has more for you than you can perform. Faith is risk.

Motivated for Risk

One of the more challenging things that many of us will go through is underestimating our ability to handle risk. We are often afraid of the consequences of our choices, which seem to outweigh the thrilling dare of trying whatever ideas we are entertaining.

Bob once read an article written in the *Harvard Business Review* that referenced a survey of CEOs' top fears.[5] The top fear they identified was "Imposter Syndrome," or the fear that someone would find them to be incompetent. These are some of the top businessmen and women in the world who are operating Fortune 500 companies.

When we give in to the idea that we aren't worthy of our position or opportunity or calling, we often stall or remain paralyzed by inaction. The cost of inaction not only stops us from growing and gaining what God has intended for us, but it also costs everyone around us, even our teams.

When we see how many millionaires in America have been bankrupt, we start to notice the pattern that to gain big we might have to lose big. We know many God-fearing businesspeople who have faced the giants of bankruptcy, foreclosure, and debt before finally breaking through to what they felt they were after with God. These challenges do not have to visit your household; as a matter of fact, we are praying this book helps you avoid them by taking healthy risks with spiritual and natural risk management. It is important, however, to see that the fear of failure often causes us to avoid real and radical success.

5   "What Are CEOs Afraid Of," *Harvard Business Review*, February 24, 2015, https://hbr.org/2015/02/what-ceos-are-afraid-of.

We've met with and talked to so many people who have great ideas, but the courage, discipline, impetus, or work ethic just isn't there. We believe risk requires getting divinely motivated with our lives. We only have one life to live. We need to grab hold of our divine assignment, bridging the tension between what is possible and impossible by actually living it out.

Overcoming fear and taking risk requires action. When we talk to people who are changing the world, their industry, or their lives, there's no difference in the initial stages of their dream. They imagine building or creating something; they don't believe it will happen, but they put one foot in front of the other.

We talk about wanting to be significant in our lives, about wanting to make a living for our families, about wanting to change the world, and we pray about it, sing about it, and dream about it. But what gives some people the impetus to actually do it? How do we give people courage to actually take risk? The biggest motivator is understanding God's heart for you and the world, understanding your purpose and that you have the power to make a difference.

God calls us to be stewards and culture transformers. If we're listening to the Father, we'll understand in our hearts that He is giving us ideas. Some of us sit with ideas and we don't do anything with them. It is time for us to step into our genius and bring transformation around us.

The Power of Counsel

A church we are both connected with has a functional marketplace entrepreneurial group that meets to do feasibility studies. Each person presents an idea, typically a business idea they are dreaming of that requires some risk. As they walk through the process of feasibility with the group, about 60 or 70 percent of the time they realize that their idea is not the risk they are wanting to take. It's not the idea they would die for, whether because the market just isn't right for it, they wouldn't make the money they want to make, or it simply wouldn't change the world the way they want to. That is the power of counsel.

One woman who went through the group had a big dream that she was ready to pursue. The group assessed everything, researched her dream for a couple of weeks, and then came together with questions, suggestions, and strategy. As they assessed and questioned different aspects of her dream, she realized it was not what she wanted to do at all. "This feels like so much work for so little payback," she said, "and it feels like I realized in just investigating it, I wouldn't want to do this at all as a career."

The practice of feasibility and counsel not only provides healthy risk assessment, but it also helps us discover where and when to take that first step of risk. Our goal is to get you to dream the biggest dream you can but also to see what things might act as blockages to the bigger dream. The more clearly you can see the dream in God's heart for you, the easier it will be to step out in risk for that dream.

Beyond the Practical

When we listen to God, He often gives us assignments and a life purpose that will not necessarily be popular with family, friends, or other people in our lives. Occasionally, we may even face the disapproval of spiritual mentors, parents, or others who would be great advisers in other circumstances. When God gives us something to believe in, it doesn't mean it's for everyone in our lives to believe in with equal fervor. Things that God asks us to do are all about risk. The only person qualified to take risks for you is you.

This means that God puts in you the promise and the story that will give you courage to take risks and to walk things out that others, even those closest to you, may not relate to. That doesn't mean your relationship with them has changed or that they aren't supportive of who you are. It means that they may not, at first, understand your journey or the risk you want to take. We see this all the time with people who move into creative career fields like arts and entertainment or fashion. Many times, their families are completely unsupportive because they just can't imagine it working for them because there is no clear process to many of those career paths.

For many careers in the arts and entertainment industry, an individual has to be discovered. There is no guarantee of finding work, no clear-cut four-year program followed by a flourishing career. This scares most of humanity, especially those who are close to us. But to those of you who have something in you to believe for, regardless of whether you have clear support from those around you, remember this: God put something inside of you, and He and all of heaven will support you. You don't need everyone's approval when you have God's approval.

Finding the Right Balance

We want to be clear here: we believe in having wise people in your life. Proverbs 11:14 (NKJV) says, "Where there is no counsel, the people fall; But in the multitude of counselors there is safety."

It is important to get validation from God and be honest with our fears and insecurities—but to the right people at the right time. That can be a mentor, a counselor, a spiritual adviser, a pastor, a trusted friend. Ultimately, however, you are the CEO of your life and it is your responsibility to take all the data you have received from wise counselors, family, and research and go to God and hear His direction for your life.

We all desire to have others share our passion and willingness to take risk in the areas we are called to. This desire can be rooted in our basic human need for encouragement, but it can also be rooted in pride, wanting people to believe in us because we don't quite yet believe in ourselves.

Other people will not necessarily align themselves with your risk until it's over, much like no mother wants to watch her child train to be a trapeze artist in their first year of practice. It is awkward and scary for someone to watch us take a risk when their heart is invested in us. It can be painful for them to watch us fall and get back up, especially when there is no guarantee of the outcome.

This gives us a relational responsibility when we take risks. It is our job to stay as connected as possible to the people we are in relationship with, even while following God forward. We have to balance that relational responsibility with our actual acts of obedience—to walk out something can be scary and unpredictable, whether for ourselves or for those around us.

When Shawn moved to L.A., he was called to start a church in the middle of a recession. Many of his spiritual mentors and friends didn't believe L.A. was a good choice because it had such a bad reputation. Some people even had a doomsday perspective over the land. Shawn had to be true to his own faith, but he also wanted to protect his relationships with those who disagreed with him. Instead of rebelling against his dissenters and jumping in with both feet, leaving everyone behind to pick up the pieces, Shawn made an appeal. He told them that if he was wrong, he would need their relationship and friendship on the other end. But if he was right, they would only have something to gain, because they would inherit the benefits of his risk taking through their relationship. He also reminded them that he would weigh their wisdom, but ultimately, he would choose to obey God.

This kept the door open to relationship, and as Shawn succeeded in L.A., the fear from some of his peers diminished. After they saw it wasn't so scary, some even softened their hearts to L.A. to the point where they ended up moving there or sending their kids there for different career opportunities. This sounds really simple and might even look foolish to some of you, but relationships can break over the risk we take for God unless we use wisdom and value them alongside our obedience to God's voice.

Take the Risk

It's time to take the risk that is in front of you. Do the feasibility, seek advisers, but learn to take the risk even when it's unpopular. Don't do it for the benefit of your career or finances as your primary motivator, but do it with and for God. Even if it turns out that it wasn't the right thing to do and you missed it, as people do every day in every possible type of career, watch Him work it out for your good. It is impossible to miss God when you fail because He is a father, and fathers are always near to their children when they make mistakes.

When you think you hear from God and it doesn't seem to work out the way you imagined, don't give up. Don't get bitter. Anyone who has ever accomplished anything that was hard or new fought through so much to get there. Sometimes part of our battle is trusting God in the unknown. Sometimes those journeys where we seemed to have failed are the birthing ground for the greatest success to come.

God is mysterious, and that part of Him won't change as you listen to His voice. There will be times when we will feel like we really know Him and other times when we will feel like we don't know Him at all. God is incredibly vast, and life is a continual journey of knowing Him and getting reacquainted with Him. But just as a child trusts their father behind the wheel of a car without ever considering the skill or knowledge required to drive, so too we have to give up our need to know everything about God's driving process. He will always get us to the destination, even if we face the impossible.

The Charge

We want to give you a commissioning. Maybe the themes in this book are brand new and you are just starting, or maybe they are very familiar reminders that are empowering your faith. Either way, our message to you is the same: We charge you to trust your ability to hear God for yourself. Just like you are responsible for reading the Word and praying, so too you are responsible for hearing His voice for your life, family, relationships, and your career in the marketplace.

We pray that you would see the thread of what God has already shown you about your life and how He already speaks to you through the world around you. We pray that God would open your eyes to see Him in the small moments, in the hard times, in the victories, and that you would feel connected to His presence as you follow Him. We pray that your life journey becomes a prophetic journey with God, where the path that He has you on is one of the ways He proves He is with you and that you know Him.

We declare over you that God wants to prosper you and give you favor in ways that you could never produce by yourself, and that others will see this and know that God is real and that He wants to meet them as well. We pray that you would find a small group of trusted advisers, that you would actively seek out counsel, that you would crave feedback and not isolate yourself. We pray that you would enjoy your career, that you would feel connected to God in it, and that you would understand your spiritual wiring as you work not just for Him but also with Him.

We pray that you will see how *He* is the hero of your story—not your strengths, your skills, your talents, but His Spirit.

We also have expectation that now that you have read this, you will take risks with Him that you would have never taken before you saw Him this way. We know that the time you are investing to know Him will pay off and that He would never put this hunger in you to hear Him in this way if He wasn't going to fulfill that hunger.

> I hear the Lord saying, "I will stay close to you,
> instructing and guiding you along the pathway for
> your life.
>
> I will advise you along the way
> and lead you forth with my eyes as your guide.
>
> So don't make it difficult; don't be stubborn
> when I take you where you've not been before.
>
> Don't make Me tug you and pull you along.
> Just come with me!" (Psalm 32:8-9, TPT)

ACTIVATION

When deciding how to step out in risk or which ideas to pursue, don't underestimate the power of counsel. There are five things we can do to push ourselves forward in the risky dreams we feel God has given us:

1. Talk to somebody in your inner circle.

2. Put together an executive summary or strategic plan so that others can see what you're talking about. Have someone review it.
3. For new products or business ideas, research market demographics and talk to people in the industry.
4. Talk to people who might potentially be investors and those who have built businesses before. It helps to understand that there is a lot of groundwork to start a business and grow it to success.
5. Investigate and research.

We are called to dream with God, and when we hear His heart, we begin to provide solutions to problems that are unsolvable. When we see what God sees, we start to think in a higher way with more substance. And when it comes time to take risk, God has placed those around us who can provide wise counsel and the knowledge we need to step out in faith.

So how do we overcome our tendency to play it safe and identify which risks are worth taking? Start by spending time with the Holy Spirit and mindfully ask these three questions, giving plenty of time to search His heart, and your own, for answers:

1. What would I do if I were being more courageous and listening more clearly to God?
2. How will inaction cost me one year from now if I do nothing?
3. Where is fear of failure holding me back from taking risks in my marketplace calling?

Whatever answers come into your mind, emotions, or spirit—listen to them! They are indicators that will help you weigh your ability to look at risks. You can only create a life of faith when you commit to partnering your actual decisions to your convictions and taking courageous action. Risk is part of the process when you listen to God, and your own heart, and explore the journey. Remember that you are wired to make huge choices based on who you are through Jesus, and you will only see this version of yourself as you read the Bible and know His Spirit.

MODERN PROPHETS

A TOOLKIT FOR EVERYONE ON HEARING GOD'S VOICE

AVAILABLE AT
BOLZMINISTRIES.COM

THE BUSINESS OF HONOR

RESTORING THE HEART OF BUSINESS

AVAILABLE AT
BOBHASSON.COM

BREAKTHROUGH

PROPHECIES, PRAYERS & DECLARATIONS

PROPHECIES, PRAYERS & DECLARATIONS
BREAKTHROUGH

SHAWN BOLZ

**LEARN MORE AT
BOLZMINISTRIES.COM**

PROVISION

PROPHECIES, PRAYERS & DECLARATIONS

PROPHECIES, PRAYERS & DECLARATIONS
PROVISION

SHAWN BOLZ

**LEARN MORE AT
BOLZMINISTRIES.COM**

KEYS TO HEAVEN'S ECONOMY

AN ANGELIC VISITATION FROM THE MINISTER OF FINANCE

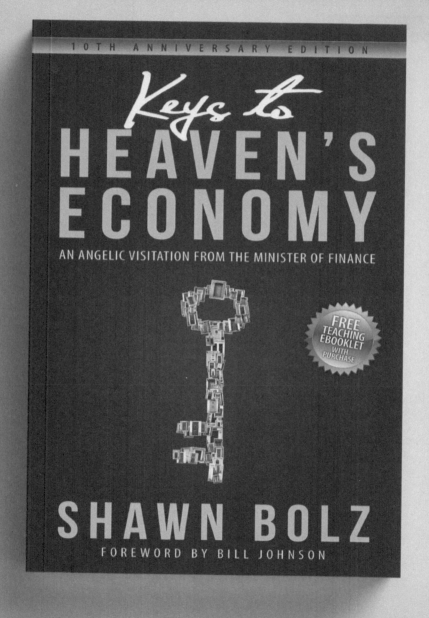

AVAILABLE AT
BOLZMINISTRIES.COM